ALONG THE LINES OF DEVOTION

ALONG THE LINES OF DEVOTION

THE BLOODSTAINED FIELD OF GETTYSBURG ON JULY 1, 1863

JAMES SMITH

FONTHILL

To my godmother, Cindy McWreath:
one of the first people to take me to
the hallowed ground and install her wisdom upon me.
We miss you!

Fonthill Media Language Policy

Fonthill Media publishes in the international English language market. One language edition is published worldwide. As there are minor differences in spelling and presentation, especially with regard to American English and British English, a policy is necessary to define which form of English to use. The Fonthill Policy is to use the form of English native to the author. James Smith was born and educated in the United States; therefore American English has been adopted in this publication.

Fonthill Media Limited
Fonthill Media LLC
www.fonthillmedia.com
office@fonthillmedia.com

First published in the United Kingdom and the United States of America 2017

British Library Cataloguing in Publication Data:
A catalogue record for this book is available from the British Library

ISBN 978-1-62545-056-2

Typeset in 10.5pt on 13pt Sabon
Printed and bound by CPI Group (UK) Ltd, Croydon, CDR0 4YY

Acknowledgments

For the past thirteen years, I have been blessed enough to travel to Gettysburg multiple times per year. In my travels, I have met a great deal of people who have helped influence me to write this book and get a better understanding of what took place on July 1, 1863, and the days leading up to it. With that, if I neglect anyone's name, I hope that you are quick to forgive me and accept my sincerest apologies.

I first want to thank my family. Without the continuous support of my father, mother, and grandmother, there is a great chance that this book would never have been written. Each time that I wanted to give up, one of you were there to help me along with it.

Randy Drais—I do not know where to start. From nearly the beginning, you were one of the greatest influences that I was blessed with to answer any questions I had while I was conducting research and gathering material and photos for this book. Without your guidance, I would never have gotten this far.

I would like to also thank Ken Rich for his continuing education that he has always shared with me while I made my visits to Gettysburg. Over the past year, you have taken me on several different battle walks that included Culp's Hill, Benner's Hill, and much more. When I had a strategical question, you were who I went to and you always had the answers I was looking for. For that, I consider myself privileged to call you my friend.

I would like to also acknowledge Chris Dean, with whom I spend several hours a day at my place of employment. Each time I felt as though I was going through a trial, you were among the first to pull me out of the slump that I fell in. When I was in the process of moving, and it did not look like I was going to realize this dream, you made me complete it by saying, "You've come too far to go back now." I cannot extend my thanks enough toward you.

The Association of Licensed Battlefield Guides, like Ray Hinchey and Paul Bailey, all of whom I have been on tours with, gave me a new understanding of the battlefield.

Hal Jespersen for his wonderful maps that he has graciously allowed me to include in this book.

I also cannot thank Valerie Testa and Cindy McWreath enough. You were the first two who took me to Gettysburg. You two first excited me with ghost stories, but once there, you could see the burning desire that I had in my eyes for the history and not the folklore. If it was not for you, there is a great chance that I would never have taken my learning to the next level. I cannot possibly thank you enough for that.

I would also like to thank Andy Hepler for helping me continue my Civil War education at such an early age. If it was not for you and your generosity of taking me to the battlefield several times a year when I was a youth, I would have lost interest and my love for the study of the Civil War might have died.

I would like to thank Katie Campbell for her work on this book's photographs and structure. Without her, I would have no idea what I would be doing. Her taking the time out of her busy schedule to sit with me and show me the ropes are beyond words to me. I am blessed to have her in my life and to have such an amazing friendship and relationship with her.

Again, if I forgot anyone, I would like to extend my sincerest apologies. In closing, I would like to thank the members of the Civil War Trust, The Friends of Gettysburg, and several other educational organizations that allowed this book to be possible. I would also like to thank several Gettysburg Military Park Rangers for showing me several locations on the battlefield that I never knew about before and the continued support they gave to me.

Contents

Introduction

The Gettysburg battlefield has the ability to capture and cultivate the imagination of both young and old. Hidden behind the beauty of the location, there is a deep heritage of family, romanticism, and bloodshed. It is of little wonder why the battlefield has the ability to draw people in and give them a passion to learn more. There is something in walking on the very fields in which many men paid forth a great sacrifice for their homes, lands, and countries. It is difficult to fathom what courage it took to march in line of battle straight at a position that may have been held by your brother. This book is designed to give you, the reader, a new basic understanding of the first day's battle and events that preceded it.

The events that led to the Battle of Gettysburg were horrible beyond words. Men from both armies were used to the hard stand-up fighting against one another on open plains. With new revolutionary military designs like the Minié ball and rifled gun barrels, war took on a deadly new face. Whereas before, men would have to march to within 100 yards of each other for their fire to have an effect, they now had to only be within 200 to 500 yards for their fire to be effective.

That is one of the things that made this war so much more deadly than other wars. The tactics remained the same, but with the technological advances, even more men would be killed and wounded.

The first shots were fired at Fort Sumter on April 12, 1861, and set in motion a clash between the Northern and Southern states and thrust them into a civil war.

The Confederates surprised the Federal troops, who were believed were just going to run after a few shots and the war would be over almost immediately. The Rebel troops won the battle at Fort Sumter, along with other victories at the First Battle of Bull Run, Second Bull Run, Fredericksburg, and Chancellorsville (just to name a few).

When the two armies converged at the Battle of Gettysburg, General Robert E. Lee had almost 70,000 men to General George G. Meade's nearly 95,000 men. General Lee moved in with aspirations to end the war with this final campaign. General George Meade had other ideas in mind. I encourage the reader to take this book on the field with them: read it slowly; study the faces that are looking back at you on the pages; ponder at the mettle and willpower of the men and the townspeople's hardships; draw your own analysis of the events that took place; and walk the same steps that men like Colonel Rufus Dawes, commander of the 6th Wisconsin Infantry Regiment, and others have taken.

Readers may purchase a book about the Battle of Gettysburg only to set it down after reading a few pages because of their lack of understanding of the military terminology or the lack of human interest stories in the book that make that battle more alive. *Along The Lines of Devotion* explains some of the basic terminology and includes a multitude of human interest stories, humorous accounts, and discusses mascots from various regiments.

On average, the Gettysburg National Military Park receives more than 1 million visitors per year. Many of these are people who have never visited the battlefield before and may have little knowledge of the battle and the countless events that took place immediately before and during the Battle of Gettysburg. This is the book for them. It goes into amazing detail without the reader feeling like he or she is being overwhelmed. I believe that the book will sell based on this principle. It is not only a good introduction for first-time visitors and readers, but also a good review for the Civil War history buff who studies the battle relentlessly. I hope you will agree.

1

Organization, Ranks, Mascots, Artillery, and Small Arms

The typical organization of the armies was Company, Regiment, Brigade, Division, Corps, and Army. At the Battle of Gettysburg, General George Meade commanded eight different Federal Corps in the Army of the Potomac. The corps commanders were Major General John F. Reynolds (First Corps), Major General Winfield S. Hancock (Second Corps), Major General Daniel E. Sickles (Third Corps), Major General George Sykes (Fifth Corps), Major General John Sedgwick (Sixth Corps), Major General Oliver O. Howard (Eleventh Corps), Major General Henry W. Slocum (Twelfth Corps), Major General Alfred Pleasonton (Cavalry Corps), and although not a corps commander, Brigadier General Robert Tyler (Artillery Reserve). In March, 1863, General Daniel Butterfield was assigned the task in designing each corps an identification badge. These would vary in shapes and color, became very popular among the troops, and were worn with pride from their time of introduction. The Federal Corps command chain stayed fairly intact throughout the battle, with the exception of the First and Third Corps, which lost their commanders during the battle.

The Confederate Army (the Army of Northern Virginia), under Commanding General Robert Lee at Gettysburg, had only three infantry corps commanders. The commanders were Lieutenant General James P. Longstreet (First Corps), Lieutenant General Richard S. Ewell (Second Corps), Lieutenant General Ambrose P. Hill (Third Corps), and, although not a corps commander, Major General Jeb Stuart (Cavalry Division). Throughout the battle, the corps command chain stayed intact.

Military Rank Organization

The following is the typical military rank structure for the armies: Private, Corporal, Sergeant, Sergeant Major, Lieutenant, Captain, Major, Lieutenant Colonel, Colonel, Brigadier General, Major General, Lieutenant General, and Commanding General.

Mascots

There are few people who visit the battlefield that realize that there were often mascots and other loved pets among the troops. As a of matter fact, according to William Fulton of the 5th Alabama Infantry Battalion, the first Confederate casualty at Gettysburg was not a soldier, but a dog that stayed with Company "A." The following are "mascot" casualties during the battle:

> Sallie Ann Jarrett (dog): One of the most popular by far is the Staffordshire bull terrier known as "Sallie" of the 11th Pennsylvania Infantry Regiment.
>
> Nellie (chicken): "Nellie" arrived with a shipment of chickens for the Confederate Army. She would eventually make her way into the open-flapped tent of none other than General Robert E. Lee in early 1862. After some thought, he decided to keep her for the continuation of laying eggs almost every morning.
>
> Major (dog): The dog named "Major" was adopted by the 10th Maine Infantry Battalion.
>
> Grace (dog): "Grace" was a beloved dog on the 1st Maryland Artillery. At the Battle of Gettysburg, during the fighting on Culp's Hill on July 3, she was "riddled with bullets." It was a sad sight for Union Brigadier General Thomas Kane, who found her and had her buried on the battlefield.[1]
>
> Traveller (horse): One of the most popular horses in the entire Civil War was "Traveller," General Robert E. Lee's horse at Gettysburg.
>
> Stonewall Jackson (dog): The Welsh terrier, known as "Stonewall," served with the Richmond Howitzers Artillery Battalion.

There are many other mascots who served their men well, including canines such as, "Robert Lee," of Troup's Artillery; "Jack," of the 102nd Pennsylvania Infantry Regiment; "Calamity," of the 28th Wisconsin Infantry Regiment; and "Old Harvey," of the 104th Ohio Infantry Regiment.

The troops undoubtedly found some comfort in the mascots among their ranks. The men found in these mascots a sense of home, and they surely provoked many memories of how things were when they were not on the front lines. These animals did their duty in more ways than one by serving in the front lines, and then serving their owners with the same dedication. Sadly, like many of the men who they served beside, they did not make it back home, but died honorably for a cause of their own.

Artillery

12-lb. Bronze Napoleon
3-inch Ordnance Rifle

"Sallie." (*Photo courtesy of Katie Campbell*)

14-lb. James Rifle
10-lb. Parrott Rifle
20-lb. Parrott Rifle
12-lb. Whitworth Rifle
12-lb. Blakely Rifle
12-lb. Howitzer

Artillery batteries typically used between eighty and 150 men to operate. This would become almost second nature to a good artillerist attempting to load the cannon. The first thing that would be done in this step-by-step process for a typically "bore loading" piece would be to lodge a bag of gunpowder down the front of the gun. Then, another artillerist would slide the projectile on top of the round and ram it down until it was seated toward the rear of the piece. After this was accomplished, a third man would set a friction primer attached to a lanyard. The mixture in the friction primer would be comprised of gunpowder and mercury in a miniature brass or copper tube. Once the lanyard was pulled, the serrated wire in which it was attached would cause friction and ultimately a spark. The spark would travel down the vent and into the powder charge, causing the cannon to go off. After the round was fired, another soldier would swab the entire length of the barrel with water in order to extinguish any still-burning residue inside that could result in an accidental discharge of the next round. As for the others, many of them would be horse holders, others would be assigned to bring up more ammunition, and still others would do other miscellaneous duties for the battery.

Due to casualties during the battle, infantrymen were often called in to help with the guns. These men would stand and hold the line as any brave artillerist would, but would also lack the skills it took to be effective artillerists. During close combat, many of the batteries would cease firing to prevent shooting into the men supporting them. If the artillerists knew that their battery was about to be overrun and lose their guns, they would "spike" the piece. To do this, an iron spike or any similar object available (like a bayonet) would be driven into the touch hole (the vent where the friction primer was inserted) to prevent the guns being used against those previously manning it.

Small Arms

Enfield Rifle
Springfield Rifle
Lorenz Rifle
Sharps Rifle
Richmond Rifle
Model 1841 Mississippi Rifle
Spencer Repeating Rifle
Fayetteville Rifle
Saxon 1857 Rifle
U.S. Model 1842 Springfield Musket
Colt Army Model 1860 Pistol
Remington Model 1858 Pistol

In the Civil War, the Springfield rifle was the most heavily used piece of weaponry carried by the typical infantryman. It was then followed by the Enfield rifle. Both rifles had the newly updated percussion lock conversion from the outdated flintlock rifle. With this update, the rifle now fired between two to four rounds per minute and were much more reliable than flintlock rifles—when damp, flint was prone to not firing.

Other innovations, such as the Spencer repeating rifle, were now coming into their own as well. Men now had the opportunity to fire at fourteen to twenty rounds per minute while still maintaining an effective range of nearly 500 yards. Unfortunately for the Spencer repeating rifle, it never truly took the place of the standard muzzle-loading rifle in time to be used much outside of some cavalry actions.

The pistols of the day were starting to take on a new face as well. Six revolving cylinders allowed the typical pistol to be fired as quickly as the soldier could draw the hammer and pull the trigger.

2

"Devotion to the Cause"

In early 1863, the Army of Northern Virginia previously had achieved victory after victory against the Army of the Potomac under Commanding General Robert E. Lee. The war, now having lasted for over two years, was proving to be even more deadly than anticipated. With the most recent victory at the Battle of Chancellorsville, the common opinion was that General Lee's army would push north for the second time in under a year.

Among those in the Confederate Army who approved of that advancement was the esteemed artillery commander under General James P. Longstreet's First Corps, Colonel Edward Porter Alexander: "Nothing gave me much concern so long as I knew that Gen. Lee was in command. I am sure there can never have been an army with more supreme confidence in its commander than that army had in Gen. Lee." In September, 1862, the two armies met head-to-head in a little country town called Sharpsburg in Maryland. There, between both armies, the casualties were staggering—almost 23,000. It was the single bloodiest day in the Civil War, and the end results of the conflict were not favorable for either side, effectively producing a stalemate across the board. The Federal Army would claim it as a victory, however, having had a substantial numerical advantage over the Confederate Army. General Robert E. Lee, like he had so many times in the past, countered every move that General George B. McClellan, who commanded the Army of the Potomac at that time, would make. When the smoke cleared over the Maryland fields, however, the Confederacy fall back into the southern states.[1]

After the Battle of Antietam, the Confederate Army won victories at the battles of Fredericksburg, Va., and Chancellorsville, Va. General Lee, known as "Marse Robert," would inflict heavy causalities upon the Army of the Potomac in the five-month span between the two battles.

At the Battle of Fredericksburg, his Confederate troops held Marye's Heights, a high rise of ground with fortified breastworks at the top, and drove the Army of the Potomac back across the backs on the river.

Robert E. Lee.
(*Photo courtesy of Library of Congress*)

During the Battle of Chancellorsville, it was much of the same feat for the Army of the Potomac. This time, a major flanking attack, led by General Thomas "Stonewall" Jackson, would cave in an entire flank of the opposing army. General Jackson would pay for it with is life, but the Army of Northern Virginia could claim yet another victory.

General Robert E. Lee was born January 19, 1807, in Westmoreland County, Virginia. He was the son of highly regarded Revolutionary War Lieutenant Colonel Henry "Light Horse Harry" Lee. At the age of eighteen, Lee would enter the United States Military Academy at West Point. Throughout his years of schooling there, Lee never accumulated a single demerit. He would finish second in his class in 1829 and was granted the rank of brevet second lieutenant of the Corps of Engineers.

Lee would go on to serve in the Mexican-American War with the rank of captain, and would distinguish himself as a great officer while leading men on the march and on reconnaissance missions to find ways to exploit weaknesses in enemy defenses. It soon became clear to Major General Winfield Scott (commander of the U.S. forces at the time) that Lee had a nose for the enemy and called him "the very finest soldier [he had] ever seen."[2]

The reputation would stay with Lee, even some twenty years later, during the Civil War. Several days before the Battle of Gettysburg commenced, on June 30, 1863, British observer Sir Arthur J. L. Fremantle met with Robert E. Lee. His description of the general reflected how he was viewed by most of the troops serving under him. Fremantle stated:

> General Lee is, almost without exception, the handsomest man of age I ever saw. He is fifty-six years old, tall, broad-shouldered, very well made, well set up—a thorough soldier in appearance; and his manners are most courteous and full of dignity. He is a perfect gentleman in every respect. I imagine no man has so few enemies, or is so universally esteemed. Throughout the South, all agree in pronouncing him to be as near perfection as man can be. He has none of the small vices, such as smoking, drinking, chewing, or swearing, and his bitterest enemy never accused him of any of the greater ones. He generally wears a well-worn long grey jacket, a high black felt hat, and blue trousers tucked into his Wellington boots.[3]

Although Winfield Scott commanded the U.S. Army at the beginning of the Civil War (in 1861), his weight and age played key factors into having influenced his resignation. General Scott would recommend Lee for the command of the U.S. Army and fill his vacant position, and on April 18, 1861, Lee would officially be offered command of the Union Army. The day before, however, Lee's home state of Virginia had seceded from the Union, and although Lee did not support the Rebellion, he also made it clear that he would never take up arms against his home state. According to historian Charles P. Roland, Lee stated: "I cannot raise my hand against my birthplace, my home, my children.... I look upon secession as anarchy. If I owned the four millions of slaves in the South I would sacrifice them all to the Union, but how can I draw my sword upon Virginia, my native state?"[4]

Later, on May 31–June, 1, 1861, at the Battle of Fair Oaks, General Joseph Johnston, who commanded the Confederate troops, would be wounded. Lee would be asked by the President of the Confederacy, Jefferson Davis, to take command of the Confederate Army, which Lee agreed to.[5]

On June 9, 1863, most of the Army of Northern Virginia was encamped near Culpeper, Virginia. Lee intently prepared his troops for another invasion into northern territory for several reasons. One reason was to elevate the pressure being caused by Federal forces around Vicksburg, Mississippi. For weeks, this city was under a constant siege and was on the brink of falling. With their advancement north, it would draw the attention away from the city and call the attention of the Federal Army. Lee also wanted to establish pressure in the north of his own. Too often, the Confederates were subject to pressures from their attackers. Now, it was the Confederacies turn to give some pressure of their own, particularly on the Pennsylvania state capital, Washington D.C., and Baltimore, MD.

On June 10, General Lee messaged Confederate President Jefferson Davis:

> Conceding to our enemies the superiority claimed by them in numbers, resources, and all the means and appliances for carrying on the war.... We should not, therefore, conceal from ourselves that our resources in men are constantly diminishing, and the disproportion in this respect between us and our enemies, if they continue united in their efforts to subjugate us, is steadily augmenting.... Its effective strength (Confederacy) varies from time to time, but the falling off in its aggregate shows that its ranks are growing weaker and that its losses are not supplied by recruits. Under these circumstances, we should neglect no honorable means of dividing and weakening our enemies, that they may feel some of the difficulties experienced by ourselves.[6]

General Lee also wanted to eventually bring on an engagement, take the war to the enemy, and defeat him on his own ground.

As evening was approaching, Federal cavalry under Major General Alfred Pleasonton's command, supported by infantry, stormed across the Rappahannock River and attacked Confederate Cavalry General J. E. B. Stuart and his men at Brandy Station. The battle raged on for about ten hours, with nearly 20,000 soldiers involved. The end result was a stalemate, with neither side really gaining anything at all in terms of captured ground. This action resulted in 907 Federal and 523 Confederate casualties, and produced the first real fight of the Gettysburg Campaign.

As the Confederate Army moved north, portions of both armies once again met a few days later at Winchester, Virginia. Orders from General Lee to Confederate Second Corps Commander General Richard S. Ewell were to advance and help "snuff out" the remaining Federals in the Shenandoah Valley, effectively clearing a way for the main body of the Confederate Army to push toward Pennsylvania. On June 13, 1863, the Battle of Second Winchester began.

"Everything was quiet until Saturday the 13th of June 1863," Lorenzo Barnhart of the 110th Ohio Infantry Regiment remembered in his reminiscences of the war. It was early morning when Ewell's force met the skirmish line of General Robert Milroy's Federal troops and drove the Federals back into their fortifications with relative ease. The fight was not over yet, however. The Federals still had an established defensive position on the heights near Winchester, while General Ewell was left to ponder his next course of action. One of Ewell's soldiers would describe their predicament by saying, "We all began to feel as if we had caught the elephant, but could not tell what to do with it."[7]

This was, in effect, a personal comeback for Ewell. In the Battle of Second Manassas, he was shot directly in the kneecap by a Minié ball. After having lain on the field for two days, the general would finally be treated, but would suffer the loss of his leg. General Ewell was now back on the field and in command of the Second Corps, replacing General Thomas "Stonewall" Jackson.

By the next day, the Federals were holding three forts—West Fort, Main (Milroy) Fort, and Star Fort—on the outskirts of town and had nearly two dozen artillery pieces. General Ewell decidedly split his force into two assault columns and used a ridge line that shadowed one of the forts as an artillery platform to support the advancement. General Jubal Early, commanding one of the divisions, wheeled his flank around to the left and attacked the West Fort, and then continued on to the next fort, all the while being supported by artillery from its elevated position.

It was nearly 6 p.m. on the 14th, and the day had passed by without much fighting aside from a sharp crack or two from a skirmisher's rifle. Some of the Federals would conclude that the Rebels must be at church "to get religion." However, hidden beneath the valley were the forces under Early, ever ready to pounce at a moment's notice.

The Confederate troops, after weaseling around into position, had found themselves in perfect accordance to assault the forts. Twenty pieces of artillery fired for nearly forty-five minutes preceding the assault. This surprised the Federal troops and caused them to scramble to find shelter and prepare for the three brigades of Confederate infantry that were forming lines in preparation to make their assault. Eventually, the Federal artillery responded to the bombardment and fired their guns with great effect, disabling several Confederate guns in the process

Finally, the first wave of the Confederate tide of infantry were being sent in to attack the northwest side of the fort. The Louisiana Tigers, composed of the 5th, 6th, 7th, 8th, and 9th Louisiana Infantry Regiments under General Harry Hays, soon stormed the West Fort. Hays was supported by troops commanded by General William "Extra Billy" Smith and Colonel Isaac E. Avery. Hand-to-hand struggles ensued and forced the Federals to either surrender or try to escape to Fort Milroy. The Federal troops abandoned their artillery pieces and, as a result, the Confederates were able to turn two of their advisories cannon on the previous attendants.

The fight was going well for the Rebel troops, but, alas, darkness loomed and the infantry fighting eventually died off, even though the Confederate artillery continued to fire against Fort Milroy. During the evening, and knowing the situation at hand was critical, General Milroy held a council of war at around 9 p.m. and decided that their 7,000 Federal troops would attempt to make a retreat during that night.

To minimize the sounds of the retreat, Milroy ordered that no wheeled pieces be taken during the retreat. That included wagons, ambulances, and artillery pieces, so he had the guns spiked and disabled, while his men devised a plan for their escape. Later that night, his men met in a valley between Star Fort and Fort Milroy and began their retreat toward Harpers Ferry (32 miles away) by way of marching along the Martinsburg Turnpike.

General Ewell had the feeling that General Milroy would attempt a night retreat and assigned General Edward "Allegheny" Johnson to flank the forts and cut off any fleeing Federals. In order to complete this task, General Johnson would have to disengage all three of his brigades and begin the march for the ambush at once. The time was growing late, and night marches were notorious for ending in confusion and disaster. The troops under Johnson did a splendid job getting into their position, and by 4 a.m., they had reached a railroad cut, which ran right next to the Martinsburg Road, where Johnson's Confederates thought they could ambush their retreating foe.

As dawn approached, Milroy's advance guard marched down the pike and right into the trap the Confederates had laid. Men began falling in scores on both sides as confusion reigned amounts the Federal troops. First New York Cavalryman James H. Stevenson would later write of the circumstance: "Our regiment was then in the very midst of the enemy, and in great danger of being cut to pieces by their infantry, who were swarming through the woods on both sides of the road."[8]

Seeing no other option, General Milroy ordered several charges to be made at the enemy. Surely, the thoughts of the Union cavalryman were on their abandoned artillery pieces back at the fort. Finally, after a few assaults were repulsed, General Milroy's troops broke and fled in every direction. General Johnson's troops captured scores of Federal prisoners and successfully cleared the area of the enemy troops. The Battle of Second Winchester, much like the first, was a Confederate victory.

According to *Harper's New Monthly Magazine*, "General Milroy estimated his whole loss at 2,000, which is probably below the truth." It was indeed below the truth. Having started the battle with about 7,000 men, estimates of only 2,000 lost leads one to believe that there was "confusion" on the part of General Milroy. General Ewell's figures, which are closer to all other reports, are probably more accurate: his telegrapher/mapmaker, Jedediah Hotchkiss, reported the figures at nearly 3,500 captured. When it was all said and done, in addition to scores of captured artillery, General Ewell's report would show 4,443 total Federal casualties.[9]

With the victory against Milroy, Confederate Captain Charles Blackford would say in a letter to his wife: "This success will give the corps more confidence in Ewell." He was a brave and proven soldier. The men would never lose the memory of their beloved General Thomas "Stonewall" Jackson, but they would grow to love and follow their new commander to hell and back.[10]

The defeat of General Milroy and his troops had not only given more momentum to the Second Corps of the Confederate Army, but also had major strategical gains. Almost immediately after the battle was over, General Ewell had his cavalry ride into the town of Chambersburg, Pennsylvania, to perform a reconnaissance while General Ewell's infantry would stay back a few miles, north of Winchester. The captured flag of General Milroy would be taken and made into a new Confederate flag and hoisted over the Main Fort. The Second Corps troops would rename the fort "Fort Jackson," dedicated to their recently slain corps commander.

The following day, on June 15, President Lincoln would call for 100,000 more volunteers to help defend the north, while the Governor of Pennsylvania Andrew Curtain would call for 50,000 himself to defend the advancing rebel foe. If there was any doubt before about war, there was none now. General Lee had begun his second great movement north and his Army of Northern Virginia would instill panic for the second time in less than a year. The Federal troops would again have to give chase and try to repel the threat to Washington, D.C., Baltimore, and Harrisburg. Losing any of these cities would result in a devastating blow to the Army of the Potomac, and would begin to force President Abraham Lincoln's political hand.

However, this was a different Army of Northern Virginia that was advancing north now. It had lost men that could not be replaced in the nine months since the last invasion. The war had seen more than four major engagements since the last invasion, and with the population in the Northern territories much higher than the Southern, recruits into the Confederate Army were much harder to come by or replace. In viewing such circumstances, it could be deemed that every man lost was a step closer to their army's defeat. Yet, this army still had their beloved General Lee, and with utmost confidence in him, the nearly 70,000 men moved at his every wish.

On June 17, General Lee used General J. E. B. Stuart's cavalry as a screen while the rest of his Confederate force advanced northward into the Shenandoah Valley and behind the Blue Ridge Mountains. With not having a clear look at the enemy's movements, Commanding General Joseph Hooker ordered Cavalry Corps Commander General Alfred Pleasonton to send one of his cavalry brigades to locate the enemy. The task was assigned to Brigadier General David M. Gregg. He would soon come in contact with the troops of the 1st, 2nd, 3rd, 4th, and 5th Virginia Cavalry Regiments temporarily commanded by Colonel Thomas T. Munford in the Loudoun Valley at an intersection of the Little River Turnpike, Ashby's Gap Turnpike, and Snicker's Gap Turnpike, thus beginning the Battle of Aldie.

Brigadier General Judson "Kilcavalry" Kilpatrick led the men of the 2nd and 4th New York, the 1st Massachusetts, and the 6th Ohio Cavalry Regiments by way of Ashby's Gap Turnpike. Around 4 p.m., the 1st Massachusetts, which was at the head of the advancing Federal cavalry, first met Munford's advanced pickets. A brief, but spirited fight ensued and the Confederate pickets fell back without much of a push by their counterparts. Joining the fighting, however, was the 5th Virginia Cavalry Regiment under Colonel Thomas Rosser. This time, it was the Federal cavalry troops' turn to fall back. However, believing that the Confederates were in retreat, the 1st Massachusetts, along with the 4th New York Cavalry, charged the still mounted troops of Colonel Munsford. This gave the thirty-two-year-old cavalry commander an opportunity that he, quite simply, could not refuse; he ordered a countercharge that had a deadly effect on the 1st Massachusetts Cavalry. Captain Charles F. Adams Jr. later wrote: "My poor men were just slaughtered and all we could do was to stand still and be shot down, while the other squadrons rallied behind us."[11]

Major Higginson of the 1st Massachusetts had his horse shot out from under him during the retreat. While the major tried to get up, a small group of his men stayed back to help protect him. This resulted in an immediate hand-to-hand altercation, and soon, the entire squad had been shot down, including Major Higginson, who took three pistol balls and a saber wound to the face. Also among the group were Captain Sargent, Lieutenant Fillebrown, Sergeant Martin, along with a private, who was also wounded in the struggle. With the dismounted sharpshooters still in support, the Confederate cavalry continued to push the 1st Massachusetts and 4th New York into a retreat of their own, and it was not long before all of the Federal force was in a retreat.

General Gregg, becoming flustered at the situation, sent the 1st Maine into action and ordered General Kilpatrick to throw the 2nd New York and 6th Ohio into the fray. By this time, however, the sound of battle also carried to the ears of the 2nd and 3rd Virginia Cavalry, who were just arriving on the field. They immediately moved to the front and became engaged with the 1st Massachusetts Cavalry. In effect, this action sandwiched the 1st Massachusetts between two enemy forces and all but trapped the regiment directly on the Snicker's Gap Turnpike.

An effort was made to charge the line of the Confederates, which had by now mostly all dismounted. Wave after wave of charging Federal cavalrymen tried to break the lines of their foes but were unsuccessful. Troops of the 1st, 4th, 5th, and other Virginia Cavalry regiments started pouring into the fight and began to cut off the 1st Massachusetts entirely. Federal support would finally arrive in the form of the 1st Maine and the 2nd New York Cavalry, which made successful charges themselves and pushed the enemy back.

The time was now about 8 p.m. and the fighting started to die down. Colonel Munford knew that he no longer had the manpower to hold to Aldie any longer and ordered his men to withdraw toward Middleburg. After the battle, dead and wounded covered the ground. It was a huge loss for the men of the 1st Massachusetts, having suffered 154 casualties. As a whole, the Federals would suffer a total of about 305 killed, missing, and wounded. Confederate Colonel Munford would later say: "I do not hesitate to say that I have never seen as many Yankees killed in the same space of ground in any fight I have ever seen, or on any battlefield in Virginia that I have been over."[12]

The Federal cavalry took comfort in the fact that they made General Munford and his troops retreat; however, the tactical victory of the battle still belonged to the Confederate troops. The Confederates were there to protect the identity and movement of their main body, and they did just that. The approximately 75,000 Confederate troops would continue their push into the northern territory while the Federal troops would have to continue to follow and attempt to find a weakness in the Confederate cavalry screen.

On the 18th, tensions continued to grow and Major General Daniel Butterfield spoke to General Pleasonton: "The General says your orders are to find out where the enemy is, if you have to lose men to do it."[13]

These words were taken quite literally by General Pleasonton, who would do whatever necessary to find out the where the elusive "Grey Fox" was heading. Pleasonton would continue to send squads of men toward the Confederate troops, and each time they would be repulsed by the screening Confederates in one facet or another. General Gregg would run into the pickets of General Stuart in the afternoon near the town of Middleburg. After a brief skirmish, the Confederates fell back west of town to higher ground. General Pleasonton wisely decided to pull Gregg and his men back to Aldie.

With so much troop movement so near the enemy, the Federals had two important aids captured who were carrying dispatches from General Pleasonton. The notes told of the questions being raised as to the movements of the Confederate forces, as this information had yet been obtained by the Federal Army. This allowed General Stuart to continue his defensive screening maneuvers against a clueless enemy.

On June 19, with tempers still soaring, General Pleasonton decided to once again probe the Confederate screen. General David Gregg would send the troops of his first cousin, Colonel John Gregg, directly at the Rebels, while General John Buford would swing his cavalrymen around to the north and skirmish with the Confederates in that area. It did not take long for the Confederates to fall back due to the superior numbers of the Federals. Soon thereafter, almost all the Confederate troops were pushed back from the town to the west at Mount Defiance, where the Confederates rallied and set up a new defensive line with nearly 3,200 men and several batteries of horse artillery.

The position was a formidable slop to aid against an attack on all sides, but General David Gregg would not be intimidated. He initiated Colonel Gregg's men, supported by General Kilpatrick's troopers, in an order to attack the Confederate stronghold. Waves of dismounted and mounted men rushed up the mountain and each time were beaten back by the unyielding men of General Stuart. Until the Union Cavalrymen caught a break when the flanks of Stuarts Calvary began to collapse. About the time that General John Buford's cavalrymen would begin to plug away at the left flank and feeling the pressure, General Stuart decidedly informed his men that now was the time to retreat. The Confederates fell back to a ridge line near the town of Upperville to continue their duty in concealing the movements of the Confederate main body.

The Federals had taken the position of Mount Defiance, but at a cost of ninety-nine men. The Confederate loss was only about forty men, yet they yielded the ground. One of the greatest blunders of the Gettysburg Campaign was the Union cavalry not following up their attack that day. The fleeing Confederates found themselves in a position in which they could continue to support the advancement of the main body of troops, delivering them another tactical victory. In essence, the Battle of Middleburg was a stalemate. The Federal troops began to take on a new realization as to the continual cavalry presence they were enduring. On June 20, it was reported by one of Colonel Alfred Duffié's men that "there [was] a considerable force of infantry behind Stuart's cavalry."[14]

This information was forwarded to General Pleasonton, who sent it to Assistant Adjutant General Seth Williams: "The infantry on this side is simply to assist Stuart." General Pleasonton went on to say: "We cannot force the gaps of the Blue Ridge in the presence of a superior force." However, there was surely going to be a fight the following day after General Pleasonton received an order from General Hooker "to move tomorrow morning with [his] entire corps against the enemy's cavalry." The order would go on to state: "Major General Meade will be instructed to detach two brigades of infantry from his corps to support this movement..."[15]

On Sunday, June 21, Adjutant General Williams would detail Major General Julius Stahel: "Stuart, with the bulk of his cavalry, is reported to have been in the rear of Middleburg yesterday, and Pleasonton will attack him in full force today."[16]

With that in mind, General Pleasonton would launch an assault near the town of Upperville. This would include two divisions of cavalry under Generals Gregg and Kilpatrick and an infantry brigade under Colonel Strong Vincent for direct support, which included the 20th Maine, 83rd Pennsylvania, 16th Michigan, and 44th New York. The reasoning behind using infantry this time was simple: General Stuart was beginning to make a habit of having his men dismounted in defensive positions behind rock walls, banks of creeks, and other fortifications. The infantry would be able to more quickly and effectively position themselves in larger masses rather than that of cavalry and match up better in combat.

Almost immediately, an artillery battle began between Battery "C," 3rd U.S. Artillery, under the command of Lieutenant William Fuller, and Captain James Hart's South Carolina Battery. Lieutenant Fuller's guns got the best of Captain Hart when a round from one of Fuller's guns damaged one of Hart's Blakely rifles. With Federal troops moving quickly toward their position, the Confederates had to abandon the artillery piece. The loss did not appease General Stuart, being the first artillery piece he had lost during the war.

With the infantry in the lead, the charge of General Buford's and General Gregg's cavalry pierced General Wade Hampton's cavalry line. A hand-to-hand struggle ensued, and the situation grew desperate. One Federal soldier said of Hampton that he was "seemingly angered, looking a veritable god of war."[17]

Captain Francis A. Donaldson of the 118th Pennsylvania described the scene: "The sabers flashed in the sun light as the men mingled together and fought in a writhing mass, cutting and slashing each other. Riderless horses ran to and fro over the fields, many of them covered with the blood of their late riders."[18]

General Stuart and his cavalry would eventually fall back towards Ashby's Gap. Some Federal troops would eventually move towards the Turnpike, but stiff fire from the Confederates forced them to retire. General Pleasonton again had his troops fall back and regroup at Aldie. Private John P. Sheahan of the 1st Maine Cavalry Regiment wrote: "General Pleasonton would drag his feet to follow up an attack on the enemy."[19]

Once again, the Confederates held their position and kept their cavalry screen intact. The lack of success drove the Federal commander's patience to the ceiling. Not only were they losing men, but also they were right back where they started. Even though the Federals had finally broken General Stuart's cavalry screen, they had almost nothing else to show for it. As it stood, the only thing that the Federal command knew for sure was that General Lee's main body was in the Shenandoah Valley and moving toward Pennsylvania. General Pleasonton would state to Adjutant General Williams: "My opinion is, that Stuart's force is kept in our front as a blind until their main force is thrown across the Potomac.... They will then turn westward toward Pittsburgh."[20]

On the Confederate side, the troops were a lot more relaxed. With the exception of General Stuart's men, the other troops were continuing their march into enemy territory. They leisured around towns and fields, buying and trading with the townsfolk from places near their temporary camps. Through all the camps littered across the countryside, thoughts of wives, sweethearts, and family filled the minds of the enduring soldiers, both north and south. General William Dorsey Pender, a Confederate division commander, wrote to his wife: "You have no idea how much out of the world this Valley seems ... and although one of the finest country['s] I ever saw, I do not like it."[21]

The next day, June 22, General Robert E. Lee began his movement into Pennsylvania with a dispatch to General Ewell: "If you are ready to move, you can do so on this order." Lee had ordered Ewell and his corps forward to collect supplies that the army could use in their invasion. During this time, the rest of the army would remain back and entertain General Hooker's Federal force. General Lee would also state to Ewell: "You would be able to accomplish as much, unmolested, as the whole army could perform with General Hooker in its front."[22]

While the spirits of the Army of Northern Virginia may have been high, the army was beginning to feel the effects of starvation and deprivation due to the poor economy of the south. Over the course of two years of fighting, much of the southern lands became barren of crop and other materials to fabricate supplies for Lee's troops. Men were beginning to march, literally, right out of their shoes and their wool uniforms were becoming shells of their former selves. Nearly half of General Lee's men were suffering from tattered uniforms and hunger. General Lee would heavily rely on the General Ewell to bring back much-needed supplies to his suffering army, saying that it would "depend upon the quantity of supplies obtained in that country whether the rest of the army can follow." Lee was basically telling Ewell that he was dictating the army's next moves. General Lee would also go on to say: "There may be enough for your command, but none for the others. Every exertion should, therefore, be made to locate and secure them." With that, General Lee made one more point clear: "If Harrisburg comes within your means, capture it."[23]

Cavalry were the Civil War's fastest movers. They were able to perform tasks in a much shorter duration that it would have taken infantrymen and with half the effort. General Stuart, being preoccupied with serving as the cavalry screen, had little time for locating the Federal position. The intelligence gathered on the Federal troops in that regard fell upon by Colonel John Singleton Mosby and his cavalry.

John Mosby.
(Photo courtesy of Library of Congress)

Also known as the "Gray Ghost," the twenty-nine-year-old had already made a reputation for himself during the war. At the Fairfax County Courthouse in March, 1863, Mosby rode up to a house that held Union General Stoughton. Once there, he and several of his men knocked loudly at the door. After a few minutes, a window above opened up and "someone asked who was there..." Mosby replied: "Fifth New York Cavalry with a dispatch for General Stoughton." Colonel Mosby later remembered: "[Once the door had opened,] I took hold of his nightshirt, whispered my name in his ear, and told him to take me to General Stoughton's room."

Once in his room, Colonel Mosby told him to get up. In confusion, General Stoughton asked by what means was transpiring: "I told him that he was a prisoner, and that he must get up quickly..." While still in the state of delirium, combined with shock and fatigued, the general made a notion to ask who he was. Colonel Mosby asked the general: "Ever heard of 'Mosby'?" The general answered in the affirmation, to which Mosby replied: "I am Mosby. Stuart's cavalry has possession of the Court House; be quick and dress." By the end of the raid, Colonel Mosby and his raiders had captured three Federal officers and about thirty men without firing a single shot.[24]

In the evening of June 22, Colonel Mosby went into the tent of General Stuart and suggested that they ride around the Federal Army. This suggestion would certainly have greatly appealed to Stuart, having done it already in the past. He would be able to create havoc among the Army of the Potomac, destroy communication lines and railroads and capture supplies, and with the armies so close to one another, it would bring distress among the troops in blue.

General Lee finally gave the order for Stuart and his cavalry to move. "He spoke of your leaving, via Hopewell Gap, and passing by the rear of the enemy," Stuart would tell Longstreet. General Lee received a dispatch from First Corps Commander General James Longstreet: "I have forwarded your letter to General Stuart with the suggestion that he pass by the enemy's rear if he thinks that he may get through."[25]

Meanwhile, the War Department and the Federal Army still had no idea what Lee's army was doing, except that it was moving northward. General Hooker would ask General Tyler if "any of the infantry [had] marched north from the Potomac?" Details were scarce and badly needed; the lack of information caused a stir in the Federal Army—they could not go much longer without knowing what the "Gray Fox" was doing.[26]

While General Lee was gearing up to send General Stuart to cover the right flank of the Confederate movement into Pennsylvania, General Hooker was attempting to find a way to get the Federal Army across the Potomac. General Hooker would tell General Henry Slocum of the Twelfth Corps: "Report as early as practicable if Noland's Ford can be used for the passage of the infantry, artillery, and the trains of your corps." The chase for the Army of Northern Virginia was on.

The 23rd was a pleasant day for the men in the Confederate Army since, the day before, they had received mail call and many of them decided to write to their loved ones back at home, including General William Dorsey Pender. Again, Pender wrote to his wife: "Gen. Lee has completely outgeneraled Hooker thus far.... It is stated on all sides that Hooker has a small army and that very much demoralized."[27]

About 5 p.m., General Lee told General Stuart: "If General Hooker's army remains inactive, you can leave two brigades to watch him, and withdraw the three others." For a third time, Stuart set off and created havoc around the Army of the Potomac. Lee did not realize that he was also taking his "ace in the hole" out of his deck of cards.[28]

For the Federal Army, all eyes and ears were focused on the enemy as they tried to determine their counterparts' next move. Reports came in from all over and placed the Confederate Army in a multitude of locations. At one point, Confederate cavalry had been reported as being as far north as Chambersburg, PA. Finally, a reliable report came through and placed the Army of Northern Virginia as being poised to cross the Potomac River and possibly directing its force towards Harrisburg, Pennsylvania. Nevertheless, General Hooker still dragged his feet and remained overly cautious and nearly inactive.

On June 24, the weather was warm and pleasant. General Stuart followed up with orders for two of his brigade commanders, General Beverly Robertson and General William "Grumble" Jones. He told him that his desire was for their brigades to remain behind and cover Ashby's Gap and Snicker's Gap. They were further instructed to assault the rear of the enemy if it was found that the enemy was leaving. "Be always on the alert," Stuart would instruct, "let nothing escape your observation, and miss no opportunity which offers to damage the enemy." General Stuart would then take his remaining three brigades of his cavalry under the command of General Wade Hampton, General Fitzhugh Lee, and Colonel John Chambliss and meet up at Salem Depot.[29]

U.S. President Abraham Lincoln would join in the topic of discussion going about the Army of the Potomac and also start to inquire about rumors of Confederate troop movements. On this date, he sent a dispatch to Major General Darius Couch, asking: "Have you any reports of the enemy moving into Pennsylvania?" General Couch replied: "Rebel cavalry are this side of Chambersburg. Scouts from Gettysburg report 7,000 at Greencastle. Deserters say A. P. Hill and Longstreet are across the Potomac; 40,000." Other reports now began to surface as well. As the Confederate Army moved northward, the southern sympathizers were running out. It would be much longer and the exact location and means of the troops would become known. It was soon also reported 30,000 Confederates were at Greencastle, Pa., and 10,000 of General Ewell's Corps between Shippensburg, Pa., and Greencastle. The numbers given were a clear indication that wherever the two opposing armies met, it would most likely be a deadly contest with high stakes. The Federal forces did not possess a small quantity of men either, as they were moving with a force of an estimated 90,000 strong in seven infantry corps, not including the cavalry.[30]

Almost immediately, there were issues for General Stuart's raid; Yankee infantry had forced the raiding party to move farther south and east than expected to avoid detection, which had been one of General Lee's stipulations. This meant that General Stuart would have to make a withdrawal to the town of Buckland to remain out of sight of the Federal infantry. If he was spotted withdrawing, while separated from the main body of force, his cavalry would be destroyed.

Meanwhile, Federal Assistant Adjutant General Seth Williams sent the following to General John F. Reynolds, commander of the First Corps: "Orders were telegraphed for you early this morning to assume command

John F. Reynolds. *(Photo courtesy of Library of Congress)*

of the Third and Eleventh Corps, in addition to your own.... All of these troops are under orders to cross the Potomac today."[31]

General Reynolds wasted little time in what he needed to do. He attempted to get as much information as possible as to the whereabouts of the Eleventh Corps and Third Corps. Quickly, he fired dispatches to the other two corps commanders in attempts to gather their locations. After their whereabouts were satisfied, General Reynolds would inspect them as they crossed the Potomac. He watched as the Eleventh Corps made their way across the Potomac River by bridge and reported: "I reached here about 11:45, and found the Eleventh Corps still crossing the bridge." This only added to his lack of confidence in those troops. The reputation of the Eleventh Corps was disgruntled among the Federal Army, primarily because it had been routed in several major battles already, including its most recent at the Battle of Chancellorsville, where General Thomas Jackson produced a massive flanking attack and drove the Eleventh Corps from the field. There was also prejudice against the men of the Eleventh Corps because it was composed of mostly immigrants from Germany.[32]

Darkness began to fall on this hot June day. The First, Third, and Eleventh Corps had crossed the Potomac River and were now in direct pursuit of the Army of Northern Virginia. Late in the evening, Assistant Adjutant General Seth Williams would notify General Reynolds at Poolesville, MD, that the Twelfth Corps was at Leesburg, VA, and would begin their march at 3 a.m. the next day. The Fifth Corps was at Aldie and would leave at 4 a.m., crossing the Potomac at the upper bridge at Edwards Ferry and Monocracy. The Second Corps, bivouacked at Gum Springs, VA, would leave at 6 a.m. and cross at the lower bridge at Edwards Ferry. The Sixth Corps, at Centerville and Fairfax, VA, would leave at 3 a.m. and, after covering the Federal Army's move northward, would follow the route of the Second Corps. The Cavalry Corps, under the command of General Pleasonton, would then cover the movement of the Federal Army until all the trains had crossed the Potomac.

The official order from Commanding General Joseph Hooker to Major General William H. French, commander of the Union Eighth Corps, as well as other corps commanders, on the evening of the 25th, was as follows: "Please order your men to have three days' rations cooked and kept on hand for the present, supplied with ammunition, prepared to march at a moment's notice."[33]

The scent of battle hung in the air like a dense haze hangs on a mountain. While the Army of the Potomac focused on the continued pursuit of Lee's army, which continued northward, capturing supplies along the way, General Ewell's Second Corps was already near Chambersburg, Pennsylvania, roughly 15 miles north of the Mason-Dixon Line. Ewell called for a meeting with his division commanders late in the day and carefully discussed his plan to spread his troops out to cover more ground in order to capture as many supplies as possible.

General Ewell divided his forces and ordered both General Edward "Allegheny" Johnson's Division and General Robert Rodes' Division to continue a northeastwardly movement toward the nearby town of Shippensburg, PA, and to put pressure on Harrisburg, the state capital of Pennsylvania. General Jubal Early's Division would now turn directly east and pass through Gettysburg on their way to York after going through a town called Gettysburg. Once at York, Early's troops were to destroy the Northern Central Railroad tracks and bridges and, if possible, continue eastward and capture or destroy the Wrightsville–Columbia Bridge, which spanned the Susquehanna River. The plan was almost perfect. As mentioned, this would have allowed Ewell to capture as many supplies as possible while also doing as much damage as possible.

As night fell on the evening of June 25, the men of both armies tried to get as much rest as they possibly could. However, with estimates of nearly 70,000 Confederate troops and 90,000 Federal troops facing an impending battle, it is hard to imagine much sleep going on by anyone. The morale of the Confederate troops was at an all-time high, and the tunes of "Dixie" and "The Bonnie Blue Flag" filled the air of the night sky. However, the Confederate troops saw a great deal of homes with American flags hanging from windows as they marched, which served as a constant reminder that they were no longer on Southern soil and were in hostile territory.

On Friday morning, June 26, General Jubal Early' troops of Ewell's Second Confederate Corps set off on the Chambersburg Pike toward Gettysburg and York. The Confederate troops first marched upon the Caledonia Iron Works, owned by Congressman Thaddeus Stevens, one of the leading abolitionists of the north. John Sweeney, who was Thaddeus Stevens' business manager, soon found General Early's troops preparing to set the entire business complex ablaze and went directly to General Early himself and pleaded to not destroy any business property. Sweeney used strong heartfelt tactics to attempt to dissuade Early, as he told of, Thaddeus Stevens would have preferred to have had his property destroyed about ten years earlier, but he was asking for it to be spared for of the sake of the others whom had grown dependent on the pay to keep their families afloat. The Confederate General, still mounted on his horse, sat and unrelentingly said: "That is not the way Yankees do business. They do not go on unless they make money. Mr. Stevens is an enemy of the South.... His property must be destroyed."[34]

With that reply, he gave orders to torch the buildings, although the houses and private property of the employees were not harmed. General Ewell later defended his actions that he took that day:

Jubal Early. (*Photo courtesy of Library of Congress*)

> Mr. Stevens, who as a member of the Federal Congress had been advocating the most vindictive measures of confiscation and devastation. I determined to destroy them. This I did on my own responsibility, as neither General Lee nor General Ewell knew I would encounter these works.[35]

General Early's men were soon again on the move and marching further eastward along the Chambersburg Pike. It had rained the night before and made the road sloppy, and progress was slower than expected. By the afternoon of June 26, the Rebels were about 1½ miles from Cashtown, PA, when word came that there was probably a Federal force of some kind at Gettysburg. Undaunted, Early and his troops continue to press on until they came upon a roadblock of felled trees in the middle of the pike. After clearing the obstruction, precautionary measures were taken by sending General John B. Gordon's Brigade of the 13th, 26th, 31st, 38th, 60th, and 61st Georgia Infantry Georgians along the pike leading into Gettysburg, while his two other brigades used another route by way of Hilton and Mummasburg in an attempt to potentially cut off the retreat of any Federal force that might indeed be at Gettysburg.

The thirty-one-year-old John B. Gordon was already a proven soldier. He hailed from Upson County, Georgia and, when the war broke out, he would be elected captain of a company of Mountaineer's known as the "Raccoon Roughs." He would later accept the position of colonel in the 6th Alabama Infantry Regiment before becoming a brigadier general in 1862. Gordon would serve gallantly until he was wounded five times at the Battle of Antietam in September, 1862. These wounds would sideline Gordon for the next several months, but he was now back in command and moving his brigade toward a small town called Gettysburg.

Gordon and his men were also accompanied by Colonel Elijah White's 35th Virginia Cavalry Battalion. With the knowledge that the enemy could be lurking around at any point, General Gordon used the forty men of White's cavalry in front as an advance guard. Thus aligned, the Confederate troops kept driving eastward through the mud towards the 750 men of the 26th Pennsylvania Emergency Militia Regiment commanded by twenty-four-year-old Colonel William W. Jennings. These troops were a direct response to Pennsylvania Governor Andrew Curtain's recent request for 50,000 troops to defend the Keystone State from the impending enemy invasion, and Company "A" was comprised mostly of young students from the Pennsylvania College (now known as Gettysburg College) located in Gettysburg.

Upon volunteering, the small and inexperienced emergency regiment had only trained for about ten days in Harrisburg at Camp Curtin and then ordered to Gettysburg, where they had only arrived on the evening of the 25th. The rain slowed through the day and the regiment was ordered to march directly west along the Chambersburg Pike and prepare to defend the town. Colonel Jennings obeyed the order, which had come from Major Granville Haller, who had been placed in overall command of the 26th Pennsylvania Emergency Militia Regiment and Randall's Cavalry. All was quiet as the men of the 26th Pennsylvania marched along the Chambersburg Pike as the rain continued to drizzle and a light fog rolled in.

After halting near Marsh Creek, a few miles outside of Gettysburg, Colonel Jennings sent a group of his best men out as pickets and established a camp in a petite field of clover. Soon thereafter, Jennings and a few of his staff rode atop a hill to observe the area and witnessed Confederate troops advancing down the road and directly at them. As described by one member of the militia, this was "the first intimation of danger which [they] received..."

Moments later, the 35th Virginia Cavalry Battalion charged the enemy skirmishers posted along a rail fence along the pike and the 26th skirmishers broke ranks almost instantly—almost without firing a single shot in return. The historian of the 35th remembered that "the battalion did not have over two hundred and fifty men in ranks, but they came with barbarian yells and smoking pistols, in such a desperate dash, that the blue-coated troopers wheeled their horses and departed."

One militia soldier remembered his fleeing comrades under the pressure of the cavalry force and "seeing all of [their] men jumping over the fences on the right, [he] followed suit." The officers were embarrassed at the conduct of the soldiers taking place. It got to the point where it was asked of Lieutenant Richards by one of his men during their retreat: "The colonel doesn't appear to have any confidence in his men. Why doesn't he try us, and then if we are whipped or misbehave, it will be time enough to run?" To this, Lieutenant Richards replied: "I guess the Colonel knows more about the matter than we do, and has good reason for his actions."[36]

The main body of the 26th Pennsylvania Emergency Militia was chased heavily after almost forty men that had been left in line as skirmishers had been captured, and confusion reigned. One soldier reported that "the officers were running around waving their swords, shouting and swearing, but no one dreamed of obeying them." The Federal line had officially broken.[37]

During the pursuit of the fleeing Federal troops, the first casualty of the Battle of Gettysburg occurred. Private George Washington Sandoe of Company "B," Bell's Independent Cavalry, was riding north along the Baltimore Pike with Private William Lightner. Suddenly, a group of White's cavalry surprised the two and ordered them to halt and surrender. Lightner immediately turned his horse around and was able to escape unharmed, but Sandoe halted and got off a shot before turning his horse around; however, it was too late and he was killed instantly with a shot through his head. His body was later returned to his parents who lived only a few miles away, and he was buried nearby at the Mount Joy Lutheran Church Cemetery.

As the 26th Pennsylvania and Bell's Independent Cavalry continued to flee, the Confederate troops nipped at the stragglers and the ends of the line, rounding up scores of prisoners. The survivors of the 26th Pennsylvania escaped back to the Henry Witmer farm, a few miles north of town, where they rested briefly before continuing onward towards York and Harrisburg.

The unsuspecting men were staggered to see the enemy forming up on a nearby slope known as Bayly's Hill. It was Colonel French's 17th Virginia Cavalry Regiment, which advanced slowly along a rail fence near a sunken lane before getting within a reasonable distance to unleash a volley. Several men fell as a result, but the inexperienced troops of the 26th Pennsylvania maintained their ground and fired a volley of their own, momentarily halting the advance of French's troopers.

Colonel Jennings instructed his men to fall back and make a stand at their new line, near the Witmer's farmhouse. Confusion set in among the troops, however, and it led to a great many more of Jennings' men being captured in their attempt to fall back. One militiaman stated that he "hastened back, readjusted [his] knapsack, and before long [they] were entirely concealed by the woods."[38]

French's cavalry did not pursue the retreating Federals. Instead, he rounded up as many prisoners as possible, including Captain Carnahan's rearguard. When the skirmish was over, the Confederates had claimed nearly 175 prisoners, of whom they stripped of all their equipment, including their shoes, and forced them to march to the rear.

The fighting, from the Confederate point of view, could not have gone any better. When General Early had received word that Gordon and White had encountered the enemy near Gettysburg, Early proceeded to send out some of Colonel William French's Cavalry "toward Gettysburg to reconnoiter." Colonel French later sent back word to General Early that they had encountered enemy troops, drove them back, and had taken many prisoners. Early quickly decided to send the rest of French's cavalry to pursue the fleeing Federal troops, while he also continued to get his infantry division to Gettysburg.

Before General Early himself arrived in town, the Rebels were beginning to ransack businesses, rob homes, and take supplies. Professor Michael Jacobs from the Pennsylvania College wrote: "Like so many savages from the wilds of the Rocky Mountains; firing their pistols, not caring whether they killed or maimed man, woman or child."[39]

The townspeople were in such a panic with the Confederate arrival that the citizens began to flee for their lives and leave their homes and places of safety. Eventually, it became clear that the Rebels would not harm the citizens, and the citizens began to calm down. Fanny Buehler wrote: "After matters had been satisfactorily arranged between our Burgess and the Rebel officers, the men settled down." Fanny Buehler stated: "Some horses were stolen, some basements were broken open and robbed, but so far as could be done, the officers controlled their men."[40]

Once in town, General Early submitted a "requisition" of sixty barrels of flour, 7,000 pounds of pork or bacon, 1,200 pounds of sugar, 1,000 pounds of salt, 100 pounds of coffee, forty bushels of onions, 1,000 pairs of shoes, 500 hats, or 10,000 dollars in money. The official demand was delivered to town council and its president. The president David Kendlehart replied to the request: "The requisition asked for cannot be given, because it is utterly impossible to comply. The quantities required are far beyond that in our possession."[41]

General Early was, to say the least, extremely dissatisfied with the response. Even after Mr. Kendlehart had offered to keep all his stores open for the Confederate troops in town and that they may ask of whatever they wanted of the store owners, it was too late; Early had to move towards York the first thing in the morning. The day's fighting had come to an end, and the Confederate Army had successfully made it into Gettysburg and dislodged the enemy from their defensive positions, driving them from the town completely. General Ewell's timetable was still being met and Early's Division would continue to move toward York while the troops of Johnson and Rodes continued towards Harrisburg only a few miles away from their position.

Other corps of both armies were on the move as well. General Longstreet's First Corps was now camped only 4 miles to the south of nearby Greencastle; General Ewell's Second Corps was nearing Carlisle; and General A. P. Hill's Third Corps was nearing Chambersburg. With the exception of a small force in Williamsport, the Army of Northern Virginia had now reached Pennsylvania, while the Federal Army was still giving chase.

On the 27th, the armies were again on the move. It seemed the entire local population along the routes were lined up along the roads to watch the troops march by. Colonel Edward P. Alexander recalled: "A few houses had U.S. flags displayed, of which our men took not the slightest notice." As the Confederates marched through Chambersburg, Colonel Alexander later made note in his recollections of a rather humorous story that involved his men:

> As we marched through Chambersburg, one of the houses, with a little garden in front, not only had a U.S. flag hanging from a window, but a

> good looking stout Dutch girl, in the porch, had a little one (flag) in her hand. She was waving this defiantly, and, as I happened to be passing, in an excess of zeal she came forward and stood in the front gate, and began to wave it almost in the faces of the men, marching on the side walk. One of the very first of these chanced to be a member of Parker's Battery with quite a reputation as a wag. He stopped square in front of her, stared at her a moment, then gave sort of jump at her and shouted 'boo.' A roar of laughter and cheers went up along the line, under which the young lady retreated to the porch.[42]

Late in the day of June 26, General Buford's cavalry would receive orders from General Alfred Pleasonton to "cross his artillery at Edwards Ferry. He will proceed with his cavalry by the way of the mouth of the Monocracy to Middletown."[43]

On June 27, Buford's two divisions of cavalry were on their way, and at 10.47 a.m., a dispatch came from General Joseph Hooker directing "that the cavalry be sent well to the advance of Frederick, in the direction of Gettysburg and Emmitsburg, and see what they can of the movements of the enemy." General John F. Reynolds reported in the afternoon that "General Ewell [was] with Early's division in person, and this column evidently directed on Gettysburg." However, General Early would move his command at first light toward East Berlin on his way to York that same morning, and he continued to move all day without hindrance of the enemy, setting a camp in the latter place that night.[44]

As night began to fall, General Early rode across the York Pike to discuss the following day's strategy with General Gordon and how to attack York in the event that it was found to be heavily defended. However, Gordon had received information that there was no enemy forces in York, and if that was indeed the case, Early and Gordon decided "to move on through to the Wrightsville and Columbia bridge and if possible, capture it."[45]

Meanwhile, General Lee, who was situated near Chambersburg, would issue General Order Number 73, which expressed pride in his men: "No troops could have displayed greater fortitude or better performed the arduous marches of the past ten days." Lee's order also reminded his men that they were in hostile territory, but were expected "to abstain with most scrupulous care from unnecessary or wanton injury to private property, and enjoins upon all officers to arrest and bring to summary punishment all who shall in any way offend against the orders on this subject."[46]

By now, both armies were moving at a rapid pace toward Gettysburg. Dispatches were being sent by both sides requesting intelligence on the small town of approximately 2,400 residents. The reports of the Confederate force being in Gettysburg on June 26 finally made it to Union officers on the evening of June 27, courtesy of the information provided by local citizens R. G. McGreary, T. J. Carson, and David McConaughy: "About 200 cavalry, one battery, and 2,000 infantry occupied Gettysburg last night, and moved this morning toward Hanover Junction..."[47]

As a result, it became quickly evident that Confederate forces were attempting to threaten Harrisburg. The Federal Army knew it had to make a move soon, and it did so on June 27 and 28. General Hooker, in an attempt to get more military troops from the President, threatened to resign if he did not get his wish. President Lincoln saw his chance to remove Hooker from command and shocked Hooker by accepting Hooker's resignation. Consequently, General Hooker issued General Order No. 66: "In conformity with the orders of the War Department dated June 27th, 1863, I relinquish the command of the Army of the Potomac." Hooker would go on to say that General George Gordon Meade would officially take over command of the Army of the Potomac, and added that Meade was a brave and accomplished officer. He concluded the General Order by stating: "With the earnest prayer that the triumphs of its arms may bring successes worth of it and the nation, I bid it farewell."[48]

The new commanding general of the Army of the Potomac was forty-eight-year-old George Gordon Meade. He was born in Spain, but moved to the United States a few years later. Meade would enroll at West Point in 1831 and graduated nineteenth in his class of fifty-six cadets in 1835.

When war broke out, Captain Meade would be one of the first to sign up to fight for Pennsylvania. On August 31, 1861, Captain Meade would become General Meade as a result of a recommendation from Pennsylvania Governor Andrew Curtain. Later in the war, Meade would take over command of the Union Fifth Corps—a position he would hold until the 28th.

It was roughly 3 a.m. on that date, when General Meade was awakened by James Hardie, an officer under Halleck, who burst through his tent. General Meade later admitted: "At first I thought that it was either to relieve or arrest me, and promptly replied to him that my conscience was clear, void of offense toward any man; I was prepared for his bad news." The officer handed a communication from Washington, D.C., over to Meade, who found "an order relieving Hooker from his command and assigning [him] to it." Meade would reiterate in a letter to his wife:

> Ah, dearest you know how reluctant we both have been to see me placed in this position, and as it appears to be God's will for some good purpose—at any rate as a soldier I had nothing to do but accept and exert my utmost abilities to command success. This, so help me God, I will.... I shall pray for strength and power to get through with the task assigned me.[49]

Although relieved that he had not been placed under arrest, General Meade realized that he had some very serious issues to resolve. Meade would be taking over an army that had been defeated at the hands of Lee time and time again. Later that same day, Meade issued General Order No. 67, which informed the Army of the Potomac that, by order of the President of the United States, Meade was now in command, replacing General Hooker immediately. The confidence Meade had in his men was reflected in his closing: "I rely upon the hearty support of my companions in arms to assist me in the discharge of the duties of the important trust which has been confided to me."[50]

With this statement, General Meade made it clear that the task at hand could not be done by only one soldier doing his duty, but that each soldier would have to do his part in preserving the Union.

On the morning of the 28th, General Jubal Early's brigades had begun to move in on York. Early would later report that "a deputation consisting of the mayor and other citizens of York came out to meet Gordon and surrender of the town." According to Major Stiles of the division, General William "Extra Billy" Smith asked one of his aides (his son, Fred) to go back to where their band was located and to "tell them first to be sure

George Meade.
(*Photo courtesy of Library of Congress*)

their drums and horns are all right and then to come up here to the front and march into town tooting 'Yankee Doodle' in their very best style."[51]

While the Confederates were marching through the town, many of the residents came outside to see the grand spectacle of enemy troops in their midst—many of the citizens had never met anyone south of the Mason–Dixon Line. Major Stiles would go on to say that as General Ewell rode through the town, he "began bowing and saluting first one side and then the other, especially every pretty girl he saw, with that manly, hearty smile..." The crowd continued to gather around the head of the column and started to slow their progress, eventually causing General William Smith to order his brigade to halt and stack arms. According to Major Stiles, General Smith did not dismount, but proceeded to give a rattling, humorous speech that both the Pennsylvanians and his own brigade applauded:

> My friends, how do you like this way of coming back into the Union? I hope you like it; I have been in favor of it for a good while. But don't misunderstand us. We are not here with any hostile intent, unless the conduct of your side shall render hostilities unavoidable.... We are not burning your houses nor butchering your children. On the contrary, we are behaving ourselves like Christian gentlemen, as we are. You see, it was getting a little warm down our way. We needed a summer outing and thought we would take it at the North instead of patronizing the Virginia springs, as we generally do.... Now, here's my brigade. I wish you knew them as I do. They are such a hospitable, whole-hearted, fascinating lot of gentlemen.... Are we not a fine set of fellows? You must admit that we are.[52]

Such a halt in the middle of a marching division of men was aggravating to General Early and other brigades behind Smith's men. General Early rode up and saw General Smith finishing his speech. General Early leaned forward and snatched General Smith by the collar of his coat, jerked him around, and said in a loud and decisive tone, "General Smith, what the devil are you about, stopping the head of the column in this cursed town?" Smith looked at Early and calmly replied, "Having a little fun, General, which is good for all of us, and at the same time teaching these people something that will be good for them and won't do us any harm."[53]

After this incident, General Early rode over to General Gordon to discuss the captured town and to repeat his orders; these orders regarded the advance to Wrightsville and the bridge over the Susquehanna River, and to prevent the bridge from being burned if at all possible. After the conversation concluded, General Early ordered Gordon's brigade to depart immediately and attempt to seize the bridge that was only about a dozen miles away. Shortly thereafter, General Early presented a list of demands on the town of York for "100,000 dollars in money, 2,000 pairs of shoes, 1,000 hats, 1,000 pairs of socks, and three days' rations of all kinds for [his] troops…" When only $28,610 dollars was eventually raised, General Early later addressed the citizens of York on June 30:

> I have abstained from burning the railroad buildings and car shops in your town because, after examination, I am satisfied that the safety of the town would be endangered; and acting in the spirit of humanity, I do not design to involve the innocent in the same punishment with the guilty. Had I applied the torch without regard to consequences, I would have pursued a course that would have been vindicated as an act of retaliation for the many authorized acts of barbarity perpetrated by your own army upon our soil. But we do not war upon women and children, and I trust the treatment you have met with at the hands of my soldiers will open your eyes to the monstrous iniquity of war waged by your government upon the people of the Confederate states, and that you will make an effort to shake off the revolting tyranny under which it is apparent to you all you are yourselves undergoing.[54]

On the afternoon of June 28, General Gordon's Brigade moved in on Wrightsville's bridge. Before reaching there, he had received some help from an unlikely source. General Gordon later wrote:

> As we moved along the street … a little girl, probably twelve years of age, ran up to my horse and handed me a large bouquet of flowers, in the center of which was a note, in delicate handwriting, purporting to give the numbers and describe the position of Union forces of Wrightsville, toward which I was advancing … from the high ridge on which this note suggest that I halt and examine the position of the Union troops, I eagerly scanned the prospect with my field-glasses.… There, in full view before us, was the town, just as described, nestling on the banks of the Susquehanna … not an inaccurate detail in that note could be discovered.[55]

After reaching the outskirts of Wrightsville, General Gordon discovered that the bridge was defended by 1,200 to 1,500 Pennsylvania militiamen. General Gordon finally determined he would shell the town. General Early reported: "He immediately took measures to dislodge the enemy, and, finding it impracticable to turn the works so as to cut off the retreat of the enemy, opened with his artillery and advanced in front…"[56]

General Gordon's plan worked; after he shelled the town and directed a frontal assault, initiating some of the defenders into a retreat, Private Isaac Bradwell of the 31st Georgia Infantry Regiment remembered his first sight of the enemy as they advanced "in skirmish formation about one hundred and fifty yards, when the fun—the old-time familiar crack of rifles—began." The Confederate troops immediately responded with a few shots of their own; these drove away a few of the defenders, but the militia still kept up their fire. Moments later, the order came down for the Rebel troops to advance on the earthworks of the enemy. The Confederate artillery still was blazing away up to the very moment of the charge.[57]

Once they reached the earthworks, the Confederate troops found that all of the militia had abandoned them and started to retreat across the bridge. Bradwell recalled that he "heard a great explosion, and looking toward the town ... saw the timbers of the bridge rising high into the blue sky and almost immediately the black smoke rising from the burning bridge..."

General Gordon seized the opportunity to try to capture as many enemy soldiers as possible and ordered his men forward toward their fleeing foes. However, when the Rebels saw the bridge in flames, they focused on saving the bridge and the citizens from the advancing flames. General Gordon "called on the citizens of Wrightsville for buckets and pails, but none were to be found." After a little time had passed, and the fire had spread, Gordon stated that "there was, however, no lack of buckets and pails a little later, when the town was on fire."[58]

General Gordon's men tried to save the town from the flames, but the conflagration continued to make headway. Eventually, kegs of gunpowder were placed under the buildings that were mostly engulfed in flames and the officers ordered the "men to put on their bayonets and force our soldiers back up the street out of the danger of the explosion." The powder was ignited and the houses collapsed in a great explosion, giving them the upper hand over the fire.[59]

In another part of town, General Gordon and his staff organized a bucket brigade "with the flank resting on the river's edge, and passing rapidly from hand-to-hand the pails of water." As General Gordon went on to say: "Thus, and thus only, was the advancing, raging fire met, and at a late hour of the night checked and conquered."[60]

As the flames died out, the Confederate troops were physically exhausted. Much of the town had been saved by their heroic acts, including the home of Mary Rewalt, who sought out General Gordon. She told him how grateful she was that her home had been saved. She invited General Gordon and his staff to her house the following morning for breakfast, to which the invitation was accepted. The next morning, as Gordon and his troops set off to return to York, he turned his thoughts to his mother and compared her to Mrs. Rewalt's hospitality:

> When I met Mrs. Rewalt in Wrightsville, the parting with my own mother was still fresh in my memory.... Holding me in her arms, her heart almost bursting with anguish, the tears running down her cheeks, she asked God to take care of me, and then said: "Go, my son; I shall never perhaps see you again, but I commit you freely to the service of your country."[61]

Meanwhile, General Early had gone to Wrightsville to see how General Gordon was doing in regard to capturing the bridge, and he found the bridge still yet smoking and burning. This was a definite setback to General Early's plan to take his troops across the bridge and attack Harrisburg from the south while General Ewell's other troops would attack from the west. Finally, the Federal Army had caught a break. General Early later stated: "This scheme, in which I think I could have been successful, was, however, thwarted by the destruction of the bridge, as there was no other means of crossing the river."[62]

In the meantime, Colonel Elijah White's Cavalry had reached Hanover Junction and destroyed two railroad bridges in the area, but had to leave one bridge intact because of enemy infantry that was rumored to be lurking in the area. Colonel William French's Cavalry had been doing the same further north and burned railroad bridges near York Haven.

In the Federal Army, General Meade issued orders for the troop movements that he desired for the next day. The First Corps were ordered to Emmitsburg, MD, and the Eleventh Corps would follow them on a parallel route to the same destination; the Twelfth Corps would rest near Taneytown, MD; the Second Corps to Frizellburg Road, near Westminster, MD; the Third Corps at Taneytown; the Fifth Corps near Union Mill; and the Sixth Corps would come up to New Windsor, MD.

The long marches that the men faced began to take a negative effect on both armies. Although far better supplied with provisions, Brigadier General and Chief Quartermaster Rufus Ingals contacted General Montgomery Meigs, the General Quartermaster of Washington, D.C.:

> General Meade is in command. We must all support him. After the late long marches in wet weather, many shoes will be needed. Will you please order forward at once 10,000 pairs of bootees and same number of socks, for issue as the corps pass here?[63]

Meanwhile, General Ewell wrote to his young wife on June 24: "The people look as sour as vinegar and I have no doubt would gladly send us all to kingdom come if they could." The Confederate Corps began to move in on towns such as Shippensburg, PA, and other locations. On the night of the 28th, General Ewell's Corps finally came to rest near Carlisle, while General Early's division rested near York.[64]

During that night, Major Moxley Sorrel of General Longstreet's staff reported: "I was roused by a detail of the provost guard bringing up a suspicious prisoner. I knew him instantly; it was (Henry) Harrison, the scout, filthy and ragged..." Harrison was the Confederacy's best chance in the absence of General Stuart's cavalry to find out the location of the Federal Army. Harrison immediately requested to see General Longstreet. First, eager to know of his findings, Harrison was questioned on the matter by Sorrel; he accurately described where the Federal forces were located and that they were marching in great numbers towards of Gettysburg. Sorrel would state that Harrison lamented that the enemy moved there "with the intention apparently of concentrating there" and also told of General Hooker being replaced by General Meade.[65]

Realizing the gravity of the situation, Major Sorrel abided by Harrison's wishes and took Harrison to General Longstreet. Upon reaching Longstreet and telling of his findings, Longstreet realized that the situation required the commanding general's immediate attention and sent Harrison with a scout to General Lee's headquarters nearby. "The General heard him with great composure and minuteness," Sorrel later explained, "It was on this, the report of a single scout ... that the army moved." General Lee now knew that the enemy was in close proximity and his troops were in danger of being unexpectedly attacked from any direction at any moment.[66]

As a result, General Lee decided to halt the advance of General Ewell's Second Corps on Harrisburg and Wrightsville: "General—I wrote you last night stating that General Hooker was reported to have crossed the Potomac.... I desire you to move in the direction of Gettysburg, via Heidlersburg, where you will have a turnpike most of the way..." The wheels of a great battle were beginning to be set into motion.[67]

On the night of the 28th, troops in both armies began to relax again, albeit temporarily, some with solemn prayers of the upcoming battle, some with thoughts of loved ones at home, some with a game of dice, and others writing letters home to families, wives, and sweethearts. One of those letters was by General Dorsey Pender, a brigade commander in General A. P. Hill's Third Corps, who wrote his last letter to his wife:

> We are in Adams Co., having marched through Franklin. If we do not succeed in accomplishing a great deal all of us will be surprised. Our men seem to be in the spirit and feel confident.... This is a most magnificent country to look at, but the most miserable people. I have yet to see a nice looking lady.... I never saw troops march as our do; they will go 15 or 20 miles a day without leaving a straggler and hoop and yell on all

> occasions. Confidence and good spirits seem to possess everyone.... Tell Turner I have a pretty pair of low patent leather shoes with heels for him.
> Your loving Husband[68]

While the common soldiers rested, the officers discussed their movements late into the night. General Abrose P. Hill's Third Corps were in Fayetteville, about 8 miles outside of Chambersburg, and were the Confederate troops closest to Gettysburg. Some commanding officers and many men probably went sleepless during that night, with fears that their time may soon be coming to an end. In addition, the upcoming battle would possibly determine the fate of the country. The men of the Army of Northern Virginia, after scoring victory after victory in the south, had now crossed over into northern territory seeking to destroy the Army of the Potomac on its own turf. The stakes for both armies could not be any higher.

As the new commander of the Army of the Potomac, General Meade was already beginning to gain the respect of his officers and men. Colonel Charles Wainwright, commander of the First Corps artillery, wrote in his diary: "Our new commander is determined not to let the grass grow under his feet." This was a pleasant change for the officers and men, who now felt they finally had the right man to guide them into battle.[69]

As night turned into the morning of June 29, orders began flying in both armies. General A. P. Hill was instructed to move his Third Corps from Chambersburg and head east towards Gettysburg. General James Longstreet also received orders to follow Hill's Corps and to then stop and encamp at Greenwood. Most of the Confederate troops, with the exception of Ewell's Second Corps, were now along the Chambersburg Pike or in its vicinity, heading towards Cashtown and Gettysburg.

The Federal Army was much more scattered throughout Maryland and Pennsylvania; the First Corps was now near Fairfield, Pennsylvania; the Second Corps was north of Middleburg, Maryland; the Third Corps and Eleventh Corps were near Emmitsburg, Maryland; the Fifth Corps was near Taneytown Maryland; the Sixth Corps was near Manchester, Maryland; and the Twelfth Corps was north of Littlestown, Pennsylvania. The marching pace in the Army of the Potomac was beginning to pick up despite the blistering summer heat as it tried to catch up with the Confederate Army.

With the men marching between 10 and 20 miles a day, it was not an uncommon sight to pass by a soldier who collapsed along the road due to heat stroke. On top of the blistering heat, Confederate troops began to impede themselves with the heavy traffic they were creating. Major Sorrel said that this was due to "many troops and trains on one road and Ewell's men breaking in on the route next day to get to their position."[70]

General Ewell began moving two of his divisions southwest from Harrisburg and Carlisle, while ordering General Early's Division to return to from Wrightsville and York. Meanwhile, Union General John Reynolds reported on Ewell's movements and attempted to try to gain other intelligence: "I have and will try from here to send some citizens over in the Valley ... to learn what they can of the enemy."[71]

Meanwhile, General J. E. B. Stuart's cavalry had destroyed the Federal communication lines out of Baltimore. By doing so, Stuart temporarily severed any direct contact that the Federal Army had with the War Department in Washington, D.C. Additionally, Stuart's cavalry captured a Federal wagon train loaded with supplies; however, during his ride around the Federal Army, Stuart had lost all contact with the main body of the Confederates. Without Stuart and his experienced troopers (with the exception of the information provided by Harrison the spy), Lee had no way of knowing what was lying in front of him nor where the Federal Army was located.

On the other hand, Federal cavalry was in constant communication with General Meade's headquarters and was almost completely intact; later that day (June 29), Federal Cavalry Corps Commander Major General Pleasonton issued Special Order No. 99:

> The First Cavalry Division [commanded by General John Buford] will move immediately on the receptive this order as follows: Two brigades and a battery by the way ... to Emmitsburg, and from thence to Gettysburg by to-morrow night.... The two brigades at Gettysburg will cover and protect the front, and communicate all information of the enemy rapidly and surely.[72]

Near the end of the day, General Meade issued another circular to the Federal Corps Commanders regarding the next day's movements. He ordered the Twelfth Corps to Littlestown (which passed the Third Corps along the Emmitsburg Road); the Fifth Corps to move between Littlestown and Westminster; the Sixth Corps were ordered to Manchester through Westminster; and the First Corps were ordered to within a few miles of Gettysburg. General Meade, unlike the many other commanding generals of the Army of the Potomac, was determined to do or die. As night fell on June 29, General Meade took time to write to his wife:

> We are marching as fast as we can to relieve Harrisburg, but have to keep a sharp lookout that the Rebels don't turn around us and get at Washington and Baltimore in our rear. They have a cavalry force in our rear, destroying railroads, etc., with the view of getting me to turn back;

> but I shall not do it. I am going straight at them, and will settle this thing one way or the other...[73]

As the sun rose on the 30th, one of General Early's couriers had been captured by General Buford's cavalry. The Confederate dispatch stated that the Confederate troops were to "get between Gettysburg and Heidlerburg.... Send in the direction of Gettysburg, and see what is there.... A small body of Yankee cavalry has made its appearance..."[74]

The captured letter made it obvious to General Buford that the location they were being sent to would be the same area that the Confederates were heading toward. During this critical time, the gods of battle were beginning to present themselves. It seemed as though there would almost certainly be a major battle and a great many lost on both sides. Men took the time to reflect on one another, thinking of home, loved ones, sweethearts, and those already passed. The soldiers knew their job was tough, but they were tough enough for the job—these were men like General John Reynolds.

General Reynolds was a forty-two-year-old Pennsylvania native and showed that he had all the makings of a great commanding officer. About two months earlier, he was offered the command of the Federal Army but he declined. Reynolds was from nearby Lancaster, Pennsylvania, and when he learned of the Confederate invasion, he was very much "inflamed at seeing the devastation of his native state." He, like many other soldiers from Pennsylvania, were now fighting on their home soil.[75]

In the Eleventh Corps, thirty-two-year-old General Oliver O. Howard was known as the "Christian General" due to his tendency to display his Christianity rather than show his generalship. Howard soon received a message from Meade stating that the enemy was moving from Chambersburg toward Gettysburg: "[He] now desires to look to his own army, and assume position for offensive or defensive, as occasion requires, or rest to the troops."[76]

General Meade also issued orders for his corps commanders for the next day: the First Corps was to head to Gettysburg; the Second Corps to Taneytown; the Third Corps to Emmitsburg; the Fifth Corps to Hanover; the Sixth Corps to Manchester; the Eleventh Corps to Gettysburg or at least within supporting distance of the First Corps; and the Twelfth Corps to Two Taverns. Meade also went on to state that it was not his intention "to wear the troops out by excessive fatigue and marches, and thus unfit them for the work they [would] be called upon to perform." The orders given showed a new direction in the leadership of the Army of the Potomac.[77]

As the troops began to move, General Meade issued a message to all of his corps commanders stating that he had "received information that the

Oliver Howard.
(Photo courtesy of Library of Congress)

enemy [were] advancing, probably in strong force, on Gettysburg ... corps commanders [were to] hold their commands in readiness at a moment's notice..." Later that day, cavalry commander General John Buford rode into Gettysburg and nearly came into contact with Confederate infantry of General A. P. Hill's Third Corps in General James J. Pettigrew's brigade, which had marched from Chambersburg and were now on Seminary Ridge on the western outskirts of Gettysburg. Upon seeing enemy cavalry heading toward their position, the Rebels halted and then pulled back toward Cashtown.[78]

Almost immediately after receiving Meade's circular, General Reynolds wrote General Butterfield that if they were to set "a defensive battle in this vicinity, that the position to be occupied is just north of the town." General Reynolds had immediately realized that the key to the battle would be the high ground. Like Reynolds, General Buford also realized the importance of the high ground. Later in the day, Buford took up his position, which he desired to hold as long as possible, until Reynolds' First Corps arrived on the battlefield. If the enemy came on him marching in a column, Buford's men would fight for as long as possible in the attempt to force the enemy to deploy into line of battle, which would help buy time for the First Corps to be brought up.[79]

General Meade sent a dispatch to Reynolds that expressed his confidence in Reynolds' decision making skills: "If, after occupying your present position, it is your judgment that you would be in better position at Emmitsburg than where you are, you can fall back without waiting for the enemy or further orders..." General Meade still did not have a clear-cut plan for the upcoming battle. He had moved troops into the best position possible and tried to get as close to the Confederate Army without provoking a fight. When intelligence had reached him that Lee was concentrating his army to the east near Gettysburg, Meade decided that he should find the best possible ground for the Army of the Potomac to fall back upon to form a defensive position. Colonel James G. Biddle wrote:

> On the night of the 30th, Meade heard that Lee was concentrating his army to meet him, and being ignorant of the country in front of him, he at once instructed his engineers to select some ground which he might occupy by rapid movements of concentration, and thus give battle on his own terms.... The general line of Pipe Clay Creek was selected.[80]

Meade directed General Sickles to move the Third Corps up to Emmitsburg. Sickles was already in hot water with Meade: the day before, Meade saw that the Third Corps were marching lazily to their position. Adjutant General Seth Williams adamantly rebuked Sickles on Meade's behalf, saying that the Third Corps was moving entirely too slow in their march, and "the favorable state of the weather was far from meeting the expectations of the commanding general..." Williams added: "You will move without delay. You will report to General Reynolds, and throw out strong pickets on the roads from Emmitsburg to Greencastle and Chambersburg."[81]

As commander of the Left Wing of the Army of the Potomac, General Reynolds would later order the Third Corps to take position near Cattail Branch, MD, near Taneytown and camp there. This directly contradicted General Meade's orders. Sickles quickly tried to remedy the situation with a dispatch to Seth Williams about the order: "It is in accordance with my written orders, received from headquarters ... but in conflict with the verbal order given me by the general commanding while on the march. Shall I move forward?"

Afterward, Captain Edward C. Baird of General Reynolds' staff restated the order Reynolds had sent to Sickles to perform. After taking a few moments to think, General Sickles explained that, "by direction of the general commanding, [he had] gone into camp [there], countermanding a previous order to go to Emmitsburg..." To satisfy both orders at once, General Sickles placed his First Division near Emmitsburg.[82]

About the same time that General Meade had issued the order that spoke of the planned defensive position at Pipe Creek, General Meade issued another order:

> The commanding general requests that previous to the engagement soon expected with the enemy, corps and all other commanding officers will address their troop, explaining to them briefly the immense issues involved in the battle. The enemy are on our soil; the whole country now looks anxiously to this army to deliver it from the presence of the foe. Homes, firesides, and domestic altars, are involved. The army has fought well heretofore; it is believed that it will fight more desperately and bravely than ever, if it is addressed in fitting terms. Corps and other commanders are authorized to order the instant death of any soldier who fails in his duty this hour.[83]

Meade knew the enemy was close, and that preserving what little motivation he had within the army was a necessity for victory in the inevitable upcoming fight.

Meanwhile, June 30 played out a little differently in the Army of Northern Virginia. General Lee's army had the upper hand in the motivation department, and since crossing into Pennsylvania, they had acquired enough supplies to feed the army without causing too much damage to the local populace. In the morning, General Longstreet had left his headquarters to meet with General Lee in Messersmith's Woods near the eastern edge of Chambersburg. Lee told Longstreet that he had decided to countermand his previous order regarding the assault on Harrisburg and instead attack the Army of the Potomac. The two discussed the day's instructions and soon departed one another.

General Longstreet's First Corps set off on the march from Chambersburg to Greenwood, a distance of only 9 miles. The slow pace was attributed to the recent rainfall, making the roads rather muddy and difficult to pass. According to Colonel Edward. P. Alexander, rather than march in mud up to their ankles, the infantry marched "alongside where they would trample broad paths in wheat…" Many of the farmers were obviously upset at the trampling of their soon-to-be harvested crops. Colonel Alexander recalled one feisty landowner while he was trying to get a drink from his well:

> It was a clear hot day, and, about noon, seeing a house with a pump on the front porch, I rode up to see if we could get a drink. The Dutch owner was on the porch when I came up…. The infantry ahead of us had not only made a path along the edge of his wheat field, but in trying to pump their canteens full of water at his well had pumped the well dry. In the meekest manner possible I asked if I could get a drink of water. He almost shouted, "No! Dere ain't no water! De well is done pump dry … I'se heard of de horrors of war before but I never see what dry was till now!"[84]

Even though they were in hostile territory, the men of the Confederacy admired the Pennsylvania farms. Colonel Alexander recalled that "big barns, and fat cattle, and fruits, and vegetables were everywhere." Even soldiers in the Federal Army were impressed. Colonel Rufus Dawes of the 6th Wisconsin Infantry regiment noted General Meade himself addressed his troops:

> It is refreshing to get out of the barren desert of Virginia into this land of thrift and plenty. Our reception in Maryland was hardly so enthusiastic as last summer but in Pennsylvania, everybody, great and small, is overjoyed at the coming of our banners.[85]

The Confederate Army continued to march toward Cashtown and Gettysburg. The main body of troops used the Chambersburg Pike, which headed them directly into the town of Gettysburg and the Federal troops were on roads of their own to meet their destiny. The war, on the Confederate level, was all personal. The South had been invaded, and remained invaded, even while this campaign was underway. In the author's opinion, General Early said it best when he stated:

> Yet this invasion was made by an army composed of men many of whose own houses had been destroyed by a most ruthless enemy, into the country of that very enemy, and many of the houses thus spared were those of the very men who had applied the torch to and ransacked the houses of the men now so forbearing; yet those who have left their mark indelibly all over the South charge the invaders of Pennsylvania and their countrymen with being barbarous, and with maltreating prisoners.[86]

Night was starting to fall across the quiet Pennsylvania farmland. For the Confederate Army, the upcoming fight would be welcomed by most of them, while the Federals felt the anguish of yet another battle playing on all their minds.

When General Lee had encamped that night, he did so near his "Old War Horse" General Longstreet. Colonel Alexander of the First Corps artillery was one of the men who encamped with Longstreet's staff, and Alexander decided to pay a visit to his old friends on General Lee's staff. As Colonel Alexander put it: "After we were in camp I remember a long visit at his headquarters to my old comrades of his staff and recall the conversation as unusually careless and jolly. Certainly there was no premonition that the next morning was to open the great Battle of the campaign."[87]

General John Buford's cavalry arrived at Gettysburg around noon on the 30th. Buford's information placed the approach of most of General

Lee's Confederate troops on the Chambersburg Pike west of town. A major problem for Buford was a numerical one since he only had about 2,900 cavalrymen against, for all he knew, the entire Army of Northern Virginia. Nevertheless, General Buford placed his two cavalry brigades facing west along the Chambersburg Pike and the Mummasburg Road, with Colonel Gamble's men facing down the Chambersburg Pike and Colonel Devin's men facing down the Mummasburg Road, spanning a distance of almost 7 miles. In Buford's opinion, these were the two roads that the enemy would most likely travel into town on. He placed Calef's Battery of six guns—four guns on the ridge facing directly down the Chambersburg Pike and the other two guns were to the rear and right—to defend a flanking attack.

Buford did not realize how serious the matter was becoming until later that night, when his scouts reported scores of enemy campfires to the west. Buford sent a message to General Reynolds: "A. P. Hill's Corps ... massed just back of Cashtown, about nine miles from this place.... A captured scout says, 'Ewell's Corps is crossing the mountains from Carlisle, Rodes' division being at Petersburg in advance.' Longstreet, from all I can learn, is still behind Hill."[88]

The night was becoming late, and General Reynolds summoned General Howard, the Eleventh Corps Commander, to his camp. There they discussed the orders he wished to take place that morning and Meade's dispatches as well. The two men studied maps of the countryside, and by the end of the evening, Reynolds made it clear to Howard that he wanted to engage the enemy at the first suitable moment.

In Buford's cavalry, the men slept on their arms. With the enemy close and supports a few miles off, the cavalry had only two options: retreat to a more favorable position or hold their ground and wait for supports to arrive—whenever that may be. However, the cavalry general would not be caught giving ground to the enemy, and he had no orders to pull back even if he wanted too. Buford rode over to Colonel Devin and spent a few hours with him discussing the situation and plans for the morning. He made a prediction that "the battle would be fought at that point, and he was sure it would be commenced in the morning, before the infantry could get up." Colonel Devin quickly replied that he would take care of all that would attack his front during the next twenty-four hours, but Buford quickly disagreed, saying, "No, you won't; they will attack you in the morning, and will come booming, skirmishers three deep. The enemy must know the importance of this position, and will strain every nerve to secure it, and if we are able to hold it we will do well."[89]

Both armies marched throughout the 30th, mostly all with one destination on their mind—Gettysburg. The Confederate Army remained mostly west of town. The Divisions of Heth and Pender of General Hill's

Corps were near Marsh Creek, about 4 miles from Gettysburg. Anderson's Division of that same corps was in Cashtown. The Divisions of McLaws and Hood of Longstreet's First Corps were near Greenwood, and Fayetteville, 16 or so miles from Gettysburg. While Pickett's Division was near Chambersburg, the Divisions of Early and Rodes of Ewell's Second Corps were near Heidlersburg, located about 10 miles from Gettysburg. Johnson's Division of the same corps remained near Greenwood. Stuart's Cavalry was still missing although he was reportedly somewhere near York and on his way.

The Federals were approaching mostly from the south and were slightly more spread out than their adversaries. Reynolds' First Corps was near Marsh Creek between Emmitsburg and Gettysburg—a distance of nearly 5 miles. The Eleventh Corps under General Howard was at Emmitsburg and about 10 miles from Gettysburg. The Third Corps under General Dan Sickles was near Bridgeport, a 12-mile march to Gettysburg. General Henry Slocum was in command of the Twelfth Corps at Littlestown, a distance of 10 miles away. Second Corps Commander General Winfield Scott Hancock and his troops were at Uniontown about 20 miles away, and the Fifth Corps under General George Sykes was at Union Mills, a distance of 16 miles away. Lastly, General John Sedgwick's Sixth Corps was about 27 miles away at Manchester. The remaining Federal cavalry was basically concentrated mostly to the east near Hanover.

During the night, General Buford sent a dispatch to General Reynolds:

> I have the honor to state the following facts: A. P. Hill's corps ... Anderson, Heth, and Pender, is massed back of Cashtown, 9 miles from this place. His pickets, composed of infantry and artillery, are in sight of mine.... Rumor says Ewell is coming over the mountains from Carlisle...[90]

One last event happened that would dictate the next day's fateful action. The Confederate Army had marched hard, supplies for the wellbeing of the men were running low, and, in some cases, men had literally walked right out of their shoes. General Heth went to his commander, General A. P. Hill, on the night of June 30 and said, "If there is no objection, I will take my division tomorrow and go to Gettysburg and get those shoes." General Hill answered, "None in the world."[91]

Those four words to allow Heth to proceed would transgress into the bloodiest battle of the Civil War.

3

"The Johnnies are Coming!"

In 1863, the town of Gettysburg was known for its hustle and bustle mentality. Its geographic location placed it in the middle of the Appalachian Mountains, although it also had flat land that allowed for crops to flourish in its fertile soil. Rocks covered the land hills of the surrounding area, along with thick swales of trees that provided shade for the abundance of cattle and livestock found throughout the outskirts of town. Militarily speaking, the lay of the land provided many advantages and disadvantages—the key was determining them and addressing them before the enemy did.

The town itself was founded by James Gettys in 1786 after purchasing several acres of land from his father, Samuel Gettys. Ten main roads ran into town, making it a place of trade and business. Two colleges also were also in operation during the time of the battle—Pennsylvania College, now known as Gettysburg College, and the Lutheran Theological Seminary. The population of the town numbered roughly 2,400 residents at the time of the battle, but many had fled due to the events that transpired a few days before and rumors of another onslaught of gray heading their way.

On the morning of July 1, 1863, soldiers of both sides awoke to a dark, ominous, red sunrise. General Lee and General Longstreet left their headquarters near Greenwood and moved toward Gettysburg. General Heth's infantry division had set off early on the march toward Gettysburg with the hope of finding much-needed supplies. Lee knew that the enemy was somewhere nearby, but the exact location still remained a mystery due to the continued absence of his chief cavalry officer, General J. E. B. Stuart.

Along the march on the Chambersburg Pike, Colonel Brickett Fry of the 13th Alabama rode towards his color bearer, Thomas Grant, and ordered him to uncase the flag. Private Elijah Boland later explained that this was "the first intimation that [they] had that [they] were about to engage the enemy."[1]

Meanwhile, waiting outside of town along the Chambersburg Pike for signs of the enemy were four Federal cavalry privates (Thomas B. Kelly,

James Hale, George Sager, and H. O. Dodge) and Corporal Eli Shafer as part of the series of defensive posts established by General Buford; these were posted about 3 miles west of town along a fence line in front of a home belonging to thirty-one-year-old Ephraim Wisler, a blacksmith local Blacksmith. The time was a little after 6 a.m. when a cloud of dust was seen on the horizon coming straight at them from a few miles away. The soldiers gazed ahead at the advancing column and knew that there was much work ahead of them.

The column of Confederates was obviously too large for a squad of dismounted cavalrymen to handle, and after failing to find any officer, Kelly rode to Herr's Tavern, where he found Lieutenant Marcellus E. Jones. Without hesitation, Kelly went to Jones and said, "The Johnnies are coming!" The lieutenant saddled up his horse and rode to the Wisler house, where he dismounted and peaked over the fence at the oncoming enemy, which was still a good way off in the distance, and began to ponder his next move.[2]

There were two approaching Confederate brigades, one under the command of General James Archer and the other under the command of General Joseph Davis. Davis, who was one of the nephews of the President of the Confederacy, was commanding a brigade for his first time.

The time was now about 7.30 a.m., and the Confederate division had steadily found its way to the awaiting Federal troops. Soon, the Federal soldiers were noticed forming upon a ridge in their front along a fence line. The 5th Alabama Battalion and companies "B," "C," and "G" of the 13th Alabama were formed into skirmish lines near an apple orchard that stood the right side of the road and advanced.[3]

Corporal Levi Shafer had no sooner made it back to the Wistler house (which the men occupied) when he witnessed the Confederate troops cross a small stone bridge spanning Marsh Creek, steadily approaching and now within 800 yards of the small cavalry detachment. At this point, Private Sager raised his carbine to fire at the oncoming grey tide; however, he was halted by Lieutenant Jones, whom quickly said, "Hold on, George, give me the honor of opening this ball." The Lieutenant picked up Corporal Shafer's carbine, rested it against the fence, and fired a round at an officer riding a white horse.[4]

Although the shot had missed its intended target, the round alerted the Confederate troops, and about 1,200 men halted in the middle of the Chambersburg Pike and deployed more skirmishers while they began to form a battle line. In addition, Major William Pegram's Artillery Battalion, which consisted of ten Napoleons, four 10-pound Parrott rifles, four 3-inch Ordnance rifles, and two 12-Pound howitzers, also halted their advance.

Major Pegram had just recently found his way back to command after contracting a serious fever. On June 30, General Lee had noticed that Pegram had returned to command his battalion and stated to General A. P. Hill: "I have good news for you; Major Pegram is up." Hill answered, "Yes, that is good news." A great notoriety given by great generals.[5]

Major Pegram, who thought the enemy force ahead was just local militia and could be driven off easily, immediately unlimbered one of his 3-inch Ordnance rifles in the middle of the road in an attempt to scatter them. On the ridge, Jones ordered his men to begin firing to keep the Confederate force at bay. Major Pegram gave the order, "Load with shrapnel shell." Just then, a local citizen ran out onto the front porch of a house where the artillery piece had been unlimbered. Sleeves rolled up, it was none other than its owner Samuel Lohr. The man frantically questioned the prepared artillerymen: "My God, you are not going to fire here, are you?" The plea went ignored, and the man ran back inside the home. One Confederate infantryman remembered: "At the word 'fire' the shell went screaming across the fields and burst high above the line of men on the hill, and thus was fired the first shot in one of the greatest battles of modern times."[6]

Upon the ridge, another local citizen stepped out of his house. It was Ephraim Wisler stepping out of the comfort of his home to witness the advancing infantry force. By this time, however, Pegram's artillery piece had been reloaded and was again ready to rain its deadly effect on the

A 3-inch Ordnance rifle. (*Photo courtesy of Katie Campbell*)

Federal troops. The cannon round went off, screamed across the sky, landed by the feet of Mr. Wisler, and covered him with dirt. Wisler was understandably terrified and shocked from this incident and quickly made his way back inside his home. Within moments, the man crawled to his bed and never again rose to his feet. He died less than a month later.

The artillery shots had been heard by many soldiers at various distances. Captain Charles Andrews, of the 3rd Georgia Infantry Regiment, wrote:

> While resting for a few moments on top of the mountain, the boom of a heavy gun was heard far to the front. Each soldier looked into the faces of his comrades, shouldered his musket, and quietly took his place in the ranks. In a few moments General Lee and his staff rode past on the way to the front. In defending the mountain, the continued sound of artillery was heard, and in coming into the open country around Cashtown clouds of smoke that floated over the troops engaged could be seen clearly.[7]

As the fighting grew more intense, the reserves of the Federal cavalry began to pour into the battle line facing the advancing foe. Each one dismounted his horse before advancing into the battle line. The Federal cavalrymen were a much smaller force than the Confederate advancing party, and eventually a withdrawal was ordered. Regimental surgeon and historian Abner Hard of the 8th Illinois Cavalry Regiment remembered: "The pickets fell back slowly, making all the resistance in their power, and arrangements were made to hold the Rebels in check until the infantry could come up."[8]

The Federal cavalrymen fell back a short distance to the next ridge line and again engaged the advancing enemy with their brisk firing. The Confederate troops took several casualties and also opened up deadly firing of their own, driving the advanced line of skirmishers from that ridge and to the next.

The Federal resistance worked and made a good fight of it, delaying the advancing enemy enough to buy time for the main body of Buford's cavalry to get into position on McPherson Ridge, which prepared the men for the main assault by General Heth's Confederates.

One of the main goals was to also allow time for the arrival of the First Corps on the battlefield. By 9 a.m., Buford's main line had become fiercely engaged. Hard wrote: "The long line of the enemy came in full view, and their batteries rained upon our men showers of shot and shell, but our brave boys stood firm ... about this time it began to be warm work."[9]

During this fighting, the Federal cavalries main line began to take casualties, which drew concerns among the troops because they were already depleted by the order for every fourth man to be a horse holder—to assist in the dismounting of cavalrymen. While the infantry had already taken their first licks across the ridge, the Confederate artillery had now come up and positioned itself along Herr's Ridge and bombarded shells at the cavalrymen. The Federals replied with a response from Lieutenant John H. Calef's Battery "A," 2nd U.S. Horse Artillery. When Calef ordered his guns to begin firing, Gun No. 233 opened the Federal counter battery attack; the other guns soon followed suit.

As the Confederate advancement towards the dismounted troops was still underway, Private William H. Moon of the 13th Alabama would write proudly of his Confederate comrades in the artillery. He stated that as soon as they had dipped below their batteries and towards a decent of a hill, their batteries opened up. He later stated: "I thought it was the sweetest music I had ever heard as the balls went whizzing just above our heads."[10]

The time was about 8 a.m. when General Reynolds' First Corps hit the Emmitsburg Road and set off for Gettysburg. For the marching troops, the prospect of an upcoming battle seemed uncertain at best. Colonel Charles Wainwright, First Corps Artillery Chief, entered in his diary that day: "We breakfasted soon after sunrise, but it rather promised then to be a quiet day for us." Wainwright, who rode over to General Reynolds and inquired of his idea of the prospects for a fight that day, listened carefully as Reynolds replied that he did not expect any and that they were only moving up so as to be within supporting distance to Buford. Knowing that the enemy force was close, he was shocked at the prospect of the assumption that no fight would occur that day.[11]

Back on McPherson Ridge, the Confederate tide was just beginning to reach the lines of dismounted Federal cavalry. As they were just beginning to break the woods line, the men could see a Federal gun become disabled. The men let out their instinctive Rebel Yell at the sight.

Partially up the hill, Private Moon marched alongside his comrade, color bearer with the 13th Alabama, Sergeant Thomas Grant. Grant was yelling like a mad man; Moon described that "he was waving the flag and hollering [*sic.*] at the top of his voice, making a fine target." Finally, Moon had enough and spoke up: "Tom if you don't stop that I will use my bayonet on you." Sergeant Grant needed no more convincing as, a few minutes late, enemy lead began whizzing by their heads and often crashed into someone near.[12]

As they advanced, the fighting grew more intense. The two brigades of Confederate infantry, along with about twenty pieces of artillery, battled with the dismounted Federal cavalry and six guns. The thunder of shells and the rattle of small arms fire did not go unnoticed by General

Reynolds as The First Corps marched closer and closer to the support of Buford's Cavalry.

Soon, while still oblivious to the fighting, a breathless cavalryman rode up and handed Reynolds a note from General Buford. After inspecting it for a few moments, the situation soon became very clear to Reynolds that their help was needed immediately. The note stated that the enemy was in their front and Buford was engaged heavily with an overwhelming force. Captain Stephen Weld, one of General Reynolds' aides, stated: "Immediately General Reynolds went into the town on a fast gallop ... where he found General Buford and the cavalry engaging the enemy." Reynolds continued on until, according to Lieutenant and aide Charles H. Veil, he "met a citizen on horseback who appeared to be much frightened." Reynolds paused his own horse and inquired of the man as to what the trouble might be; the man stated "that [their] Cavalry was fighting."[13]

On Seminary Ridge, General Buford glanced over the field to find a commanding position from which to better observe the battle. The cupola of the Lutheran Theological Seminary was the most obvious choice for Buford, and he joined Lieutenant Aaron B. Jerome, of the Signal Corps, who himself had actually been up there as early as 7 a.m. to view over the battle and keep a sharp eye out for the First Corps.

Upon reaching this point, the view was just as they planned it. They could keep one eye on the battlefield and one eye open for Reynolds. The steep height offered a commanding view of the whole area and the heights on the other side of town.

A little after 10 a.m., Lieutenant Jerome noticed a small column of Federal troops off in the distance. He hastily pointed it out to General Buford, who sighed deeply knowing relief was on its way. Buford stated: "Now we can hold this place!" General Buford then issued a dispatch to General Meade, informing him of their current situation:

> The enemy's force (A. P. Hill's) are advancing on me at this point, and driving my pickets and skirmishers very rapidly.... General Reynolds is advancing, and is within .3 miles of this point with his leading division. I am positive that the whole of A. P. Hill's force is advancing.[14]

General Buford and Lieutenant Jerome watched from the cupola as General Reynolds and his staff galloped towards them. Arriving just below them, General Reynolds steadied his horse and yelled up, asking, "What's the matter, John?" to which Buford replied, "The devil's to pay!" Reynolds, seeing the smoke from the battle, said, "I hope you can hold out until my corps comes up." Buford quickly said, "I reckon I can." The agreeable

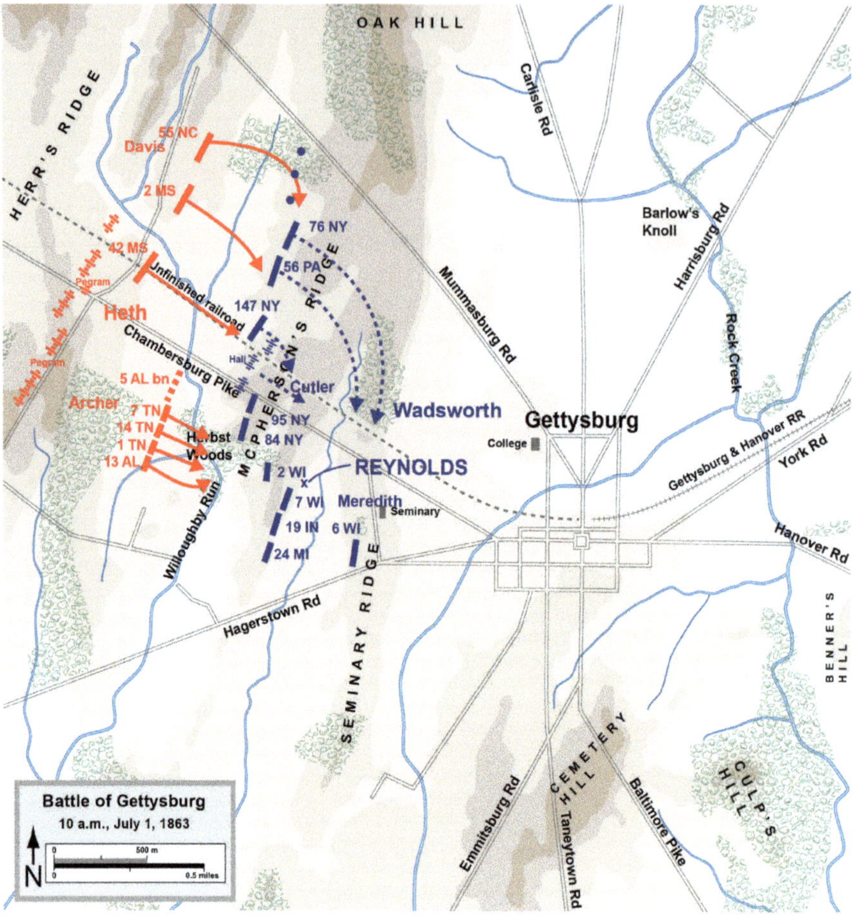

July 1, 10 a.m. (*Map by Hal Jespersen, www.cwmaps.com*)

Reynolds, sharply replied, "Let's go and see." This statement by Reynolds did not sit well with Buford. The cavalry officer quickly forewarned the corps commander of the dangers of moving too close to the fighting front, which Reynolds just laughed off, pressing towards the fight.[15]

Halfway to the Federal line, Reynolds turned to his aide, Stephen Weld, and told him to ride at once with utmost speed to General Meade and report that "the enemy were coming on in strong force, and that he was afraid they would get the heights on the other side of the town before he could; that he would fight them all through the town, however, and keep them back as long as possible."[16]

Moments later, Weld was off to give the report to Meade in Taneytown, MD, while Buford and Reynolds were discussing going over how the conflict was playing itself out near the battle line, when a frantic Colonel Gamble quickly rode up to Reynolds. "Hurry up, General, Hurry up! They are breaking our line!" Gamble said. Some reassurance was delivered to Gamble after Reynolds spoke to him and the matter calmed itself down.[17]

General Reynolds knew that his First Corps was still a short distance off. The situation called for immediate attention, however. Therefore, he ordered General Buford "to hold the enemy in check as long as possible, to keep them from getting into town..." Shortly thereafter, Reynolds also ordered for the Third and the Eleventh Corps to come up as fast as possible to help in defending the ground beyond the town. He knew that if the enemy captured the heights first, the war would soon be over—and not in their favor.[18]

On the Confederate side, General Lee also began preparing as by sending orders to Brigadier General J. D. Imboden and his cavalry; he stated: "Upon arriving at Chambersburg today, I desire you to relieve General Pickett, who will then move forward to this place." Lee would go on to instruct Imboden: "Obtain all the flour that you can load in your wagons from the mills in your vicinity.... It will be necessary for you to have your men well together and always on the alert, and to pay strict attention to the safety of the trains ... upon the safety of which the operations of this army depend." With that order, General Lee began to push all his troops towards the town of Gettysburg. Even though, only a few days before, Lee advised that he would much rather have fought at Cashtown, using the mountains as a place to withdraw in the event of their defeat.[19]

Back towards McPherson Ridge, General Reynolds began to take defensive measures. In the event of getting pushed back from their position, he ordered his staff escort to tear down the fences, which ran along the Emmitsburg Road, to make it easier to retreat and get to higher ground and assume a new defensive position. Reynolds and his staff then rode to the head of their advancing column, commanded by fifty-five-year-old General James S. Wadsworth, and order them into line of battle on McPherson Ridge.

By this time, the Confederate advance had stalled due to the hard-nosed fighting tactics of the Federal cavalrymen, which forced them into line of battle. The Confederates deployed two brigades (Archer's and Davis') to the front and held two brigades in reserve (Brockenbrough's and Pettigrew's). The brigade under General James Jay Archer consisted of the 5th Alabama Infantry Battalion, 13th Alabama Infantry Regiment, and the 1st, 7th, and 14th Tennessee Infantry Regiments. General Joseph R. Davis' troops consisted of the 2nd and 42nd Mississippi Infantry Regiments and the 55th North Carolina Infantry Regiment, and they were placed a little farther north with their left resting near the John Forney house along the Mummasburg Road.

The dismounted cavalry lines were almost to their breaking point on McPherson Ridge as the brigades of General Wadsworth's First Division of the First Corps arrived. The Second Brigade was commanded by General Lysander Cutler, and consisted of the 14th Brooklyn, 76th, 95th, and 147th New York Infantry Regiments and the 56th Pennsylvania Infantry Regiment. Behind Cutler's Brigade

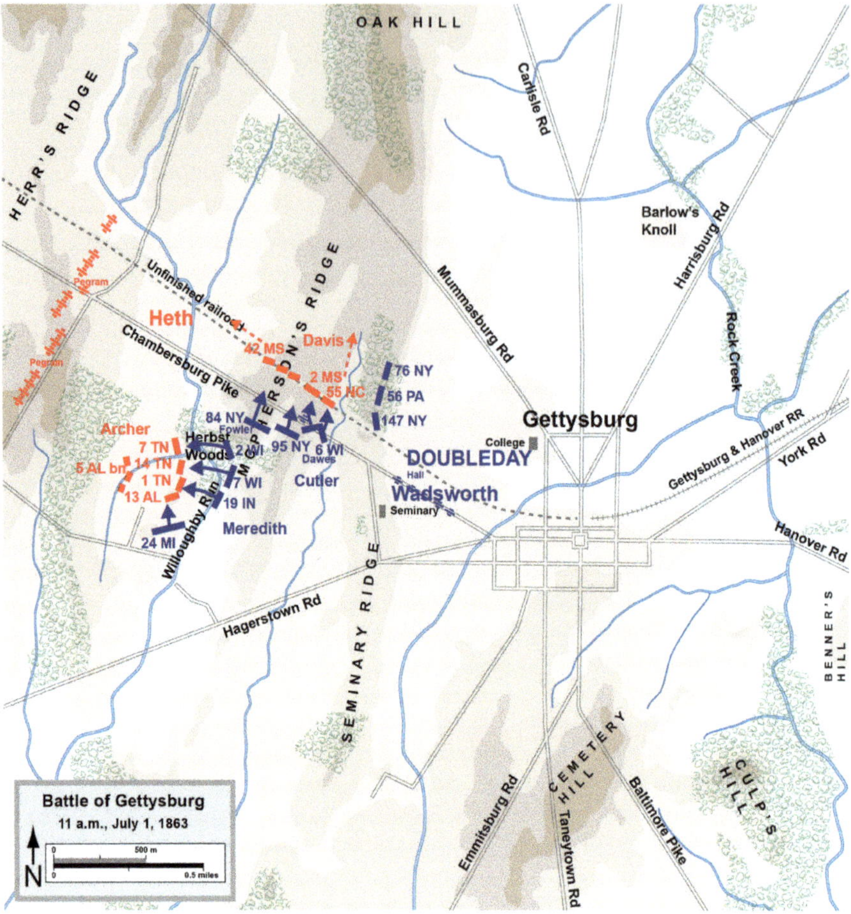

July 1, 11 a.m. (*Map by Hal Jespersen, www.cwmaps.com*)

came North Carolina native General Solomon "Long Sol" Meredith's First Brigade (his nickname reflected his towering height of 6 feet 7 inches). Nicknamed the "Iron Brigade," primarily because of their actions during the Battle of South Mountain, Meredith's brigade was mostly composed of troops from Western states and consisted of the 19th Indiana Infantry Regiment, 24th Michigan Infantry Regiment, and the 2nd, 6th, and 7th Wisconsin Infantry Regiments.

Also soon coming up for the Federal Army were the other divisions of the First Corps. Colonel Wainwright, who commanded the First Corps Artillery, remembered speaking with General Abner Doublday: "We were just speaking of General Meade's promotion and Doublday was just saying that Sykes was his junior, and they ought to give him a corps, when my attention was called to the smoke of shells bursting in the air ... which we supposed to be from Buford's cavalry. In a few minutes, however, an officer ... came up with orders for us to push on as fast as possible..."[20]

As the 6th Wisconsin Infantry Regiment approached the Lutheran Theological Seminary, Colonel Dawes recalled that "all were in the highest of spirits." To further boost their morale, Dawes had the regimental flags unfurled and ordered Drum Major R. N. Smith to play the song "The Campbell's are coming."[21]

Out in the front of the division, Cutler's Brigade turned toward the sound of battle, which had been emanating from Seminary Ridge, and reached the crest first. They were followed close behind by Meredith's Brigade. Lieutenant Gilbert M. Woodward of General Meredith's staff soon rode over to Colonel Dawes and said, "Colonel, form your line, and prepare for action." This is all that Dawes needed to hear; he immediately turned and gave the order to his men to advance at a double quick and to load their muskets as they ran.[22]

Further to the west, General Reynolds ordered Hall's 2nd Maine Battery of six 3-inch Ordinance rifles to replace the heavily outgunned horse artillery along the Chambersburg Pike to cover the deployment of the Federal infantry. Reynolds rode to General Wadsworth and ordered him to split Cutler's Brigade, with half to be deployed in the unfinished railroad cut and the other half to the other side of the cut. The other regiments in the brigade were to stay back and protect against any attackers from Herbst Woods or an attack from the opposite flank.

Meredith's men were deployed near the crest of the ridge and ordered to take the place of Colonel Gamble's cavalrymen, who had just begun to withdraw due partly to being almost out of ammunition. However, the work that had been done by the Federal cavalry was not enough for one man in the 8th Illinois Cavalry Regiment:

> As the cavalry skirmishers fell back, one man, either not hearing the command or determined not to yield, at first stood his ground, then lay down in the grass until the enemy's line was nearly upon him, when he arose he cried out at the top of his voice, "Come on-we have them." General Buford didn't know if the Rebels were astonished at his madness, or thought he was an officer leading on a host, we know not, but their line faltered...[23]

The men of the "Iron Brigade" were some of the first infantry troops to meet the enemy on the field that day. They wore distinctive black Hardee hats, complete with a black ostrich feather, one side of the brim of the hat pinned up, also sporting a brass eagle pin.

At this moment, the Confederates were claiming the day to be a victory. However, they had no idea what laid on the other side of McPherson's Ridge. Once the Iron Brigade struck Archer's line, the Rebels realized they were in for a fight. As one Confederate exclaimed: "There are those damned black-hatted fellows again. 'Taint no militia. It's the Army of the Potomac.'"[24]

4

The First Corps Arrives

One of the advantages the Army of the Potomac had over the Army of Northern Virginia was the lay of the land. Upon the advancement down the Chambersburg Pike, the hills and woodlots were able conceal what may have been lying in wait on the other side. Likewise, McPherson's Ridge had this topography, and when the First Corps arrived, their position had yet to become known. Therefore, when the support for General Buford's cavalry came rushing into the fray, it may be said that it came as a surprise to General James Archer's Brigade, who was probably overly aggressive from the start. Archer went from outnumbering the enemy (as he took almost 1,200 men into battle alone) to now being outnumbered and he never knew it until it was too late.

The Iron Brigade had been deployed on the other side of the John Herbst Woods, just south of the Edward McPherson farmhouses. Records show that, during the time of battle, the McPherson family did not occupy the farmstead, and it was instead rented to the family of John Slentz, who had already begun to seek shelter in town. Though they did not know it, much of their rented buildings and home goods would be tarnished by the horrors of war. Much of their possessions would be ransacked for the use of makeshift hospital supplies, while the floors would become stained with the blood of the dead and wounded.

Though the supports for Colonel William Gamble's cavalry arrived on behalf of General Reynolds, the Confederate troops still had momentum and were making a strong push through the woods in pursuit of the fleeing Federal cavalrymen. "The Genl ordered our troops to advance near to the top of the ridge and lay down," Sergeant Charles Veil, orderly of Reynolds, would later write, adding, "The enemy advanced up at the other side of the ridge and both lines met near the top."[1]

The action for the First Corps commenced rapidly when the enemy came into full view. The fighting was intense, but General Reynolds remained mounted on his horse. He soon noticed the enemy was beginning to advance in an attempt to outflank his position. Reynolds quickly drew his sword and ordered the 2nd Wisconsin Infantry Regiment, who had been positioned in the rear of the brigade, "forward into line at a double quick." However, the charge ended up being unsuccessful and, worse, the enemy was "not much more than 60 paces from where the Genl. [Reynolds] was."

The firing was severe during this brief standoff between the 2nd Wisconsin and Confederate troops. Reynolds turned in his saddle to see if any of the troops followed, and shouted, "Forward men, forward for God's sake and drive those fellows out of those woods!" Lieutenant Veil remembered when tragedy struck a few moments later:

> The Genl turned to look toward the Seminary (I suppose to see if the other troops were coming on) and as he did so, a minnie ball struck him in the back of the neck and he fell from his horse dead.... He never spoke a word, or moved a muscle after he was struck. I have seen many men killed in action, but never saw a ball do its work so instantly as did the ball which struck General Reynolds, a man who knew not what fear or danger was; in a word was one of our very best Generals.... The Genl fell on his left side. I turned him on his back, glanced over him but could see no wound except a bruise above his left eye. We were under the impression that he was only stunned...[2]

General Reynolds was carried by Captain Mitchell, Captain Baird, and Sergeant Veil to the Seminary a short distance away, while the Federals began to file into the woods "*en echelon*." When the small party carrying the body rendered it halfway between the spot he fell and the Seminary, Reynolds gave an apparent sign of life. According to Veil, "he gasped a little and [he] thought [Reynolds] was coming to his senses." The men set down the general and Veil attempted to give him water from his canteen, "but he would not drink, it was his last struggle."[3]

Colonel Wainwright had just arrived near the Seminary when he had learned of the fate of Reynolds. Wadsworth approached and "merely said, 'The General is killed; Reynolds is dead.'" The greatly disheartened Colonel Wainwright later wrote: "Shortly after I met his body being brought off. I halted and uncovered as he passed; it was all there was time for..." With Reynolds dead, General Abner Doubleday now commanded the First Corps.[4]

General Archer now found his brigade in a bad position. Bill Arp of the 13th Alabama was heard to exclaim, "We had Yankees on the front, Yankees on the flanks, and soon Yankees behind us." Once the Federal cavalry line broke for the rear, they swung around and gave some fire to the rebel flanks, killing and wounding a great many of them.[5]

The attack from the Iron Brigade had near come full circle. Regiment after regiment rushed into battle, while the 6th Wisconsin was held in

Abner Doubleday.
(Photo courtesy of Library of Congress)

reserve and, eventually, the full brigade was committed to the fight. During their flanking maneuver, the First Corps, First Division, First Brigade, pushed Archer's Brigade across the run and partly up the next slope. One of these men, in full retreat, was General Archer, who unsuccessfully attempted to elude a pursuing Federal wave of infantry. The 2nd Wisconsin was now being supported by the 7th Wisconsin and, soon thereafter, the 19th Indiana and 24th Michigan, forcing the Confederate troops into a pinch point.

W. H. Bird, the 13th Alabama Regimental historian, who was a private at the time, recalled the withdrawal:

> So on we went down the hill (toward Willoughby Run) We finally arrived at the ravine, crossed the clearest stream; pebbles on the bottom nearly knee deep, rose a rugged step bluff, and entered a wheat field about a half mile of Gettysburg ... when all of sudden a heavy line of battle rose out of the wheat and poured a volley into our ranks. It wavered and they charged us, and we fell back to the ravine again, and before we could possibly rally, it seemed to me there were 20,000 Yanks down in among us hollowing surrender.[6]

The surprised Confederate forces began to throw down their firearms in scores. Private Bird, however, continued to fight before finally being compelled to surrender. During this struggle, Lieutenant Pond of the 13th Alabama was told to surrender by "a private or two." The confused lieutenant looked at Bird, who was standing but a few paces away, and said, "Bird, what in the hell shall I do?" The private exclaimed, "I don't see what you can do, but surrender..." The reluctant officer threw his sword down on the ground at the Federal's feet. The 20,000 "Yanks" that Bird had seen were actually the 24th Michigan, who had swung around the flank of Archer's Brigade and delivered a murderous fire. After a short time, the 24th Michigan advanced with the 19th Indiana, laying claim to nearly 100 captured men.[7]

Private Patrick Mahoney of the 2nd Wisconsin became caught up in the smoke and chaos that a battlefield produces. The ranks of the Confederates looked like a huge mass of confusion. Lieutenant Colonel S. G. Shepard of the 7th Tennessee Infantry Regiment reported: "I saw General Archer ... and he appeared to be very much exhausted with fatigue." Before the fighting broke out, he displayed his unwillingness to carry out the attack so far out in front of his support. During this whirlpool of smoke and fire, Mahoney took notice to the fleeing Confederate officer attempting to make his escape. The persistent private followed the general into the bushes and, before the end of foray, made the personal capture of General James Jay Archer.

As the general's presence was noticed by Lieutenant D. B. Daily, he approached Archer and exclaimed, "I'll relieve you of that sword." The general reluctantly handed it over to Daily and was sent to the rear. General Abner Doubleday, now in command of the First Corps and the battlefield, gazed at the captured soldiers in his rear position. Upon looking them over, he thought he had spotted a familiar face. Riding over to Archer, he said, "Good morning, Archer, how are you? I am glad to see you." The captured officer was much less enthused about the meeting between old West Point classmates and replied, "Well, I am not glad to see you by a damn sight!" The slightly shocked and embarrassed Doubleday shrugged his shoulders and fixed himself in his saddle. "Take him to the rear; take him to the rear!" he exclaimed.[8]

The Federals' successes came as a surprise to General Heth, who later admitted that he "was ignorant what force was at or near Gettysburg..." General Heth was originally under the assumption that he only had to scatter a few dismounted cavalrymen at the very most. Unlike his Federal counterparts, he had no idea that the entire opposing army was merely a few miles away. He still had an ace hidden in his sleeve in the brigade of General Joseph Davis and two other brigades in reserve. Now commanded by Colonel Brickett Fry, Archer's Brigade's day of fighting had concluded.[9]

With the Federals holding the upper hand in Herbst Woods after driving off General Archer's Brigade, the same could not be said on the opposite side of the Chambersburg Pike, where, with the exception of the 11th Mississippi having been detached to guard supply trains in the rear, General Joseph R. Davis' Brigade was deployed. Earlier in the day, General Reynolds personally instructed General James Wadsworth, commander of the First Division in the First Corps, to place most of the 1,600 troops in General Lysander Cutler's Second Brigade on the opposite side of the unfinished railroad cut (the 56th New York Infantry Regiment, 76th New York Infantry Regiment, and 147th New York Infantry Regiment); he also directed two other regiments (the 14th Brooklyn Infantry Regiment and the 95th New York Infantry Regiment) to be held back in support. The Confederate troops came from the direction of the Bender farm, about 1 mile outside of town, and came deployed in a line of battle. Davis threw out skirmishers in front of his brigade and boldly marched his men into the jaws of death to meet General Cutler's brigade.

It was now about 10.30 a.m. as the Confederate troops made their way across the open Pennsylvanian fields. Not long into their advance, the rebel force began to notice the solid line of blue upon the crest of the ridge. They continued about another mile when skirmishers from both sides began trading shots with each other in the tall wheat fields in front of their position. The Federal skirmish line was quickly driven back to the main body. Every man knew that "the engagement soon became very warm."[10]

In line of battle, the troops of the 55th North Carolina Infantry Regiment marched around the flank of the 76th New York, which had been placed on the right of the Federal brigade, and contested that flank, while the troops of the 2nd Mississippi came straight on against the 56th Pennsylvania. Finally, the troops of the 42nd Mississippi attacked along the railroad cut towards the 147th New York.

After a few minutes of hard stand-up fighting, the order of charge rang along the Confederate line, which was "promptly obeyed." Captain Leander G. Woolard of Company "B" of the 42nd Mississippi remembered the advance:

> Just as we were charging them, we came to a top of a hill in a wheat field and behold a regiment of the blue bellies immediately in front and not over 100 yards from me. Just as they leveled their guns to fire, quick as thought I gave the command to 'lay down' and a shower of balls passed over our heads...

Once ordered up, the 42nd fired their own lead, inflicting heavy casualties on the Yankees.[11]

The rounds continued to hiss through the air, and Hall's unrelenting artillery guns continued to sing their songs. Captain Woolard noticed that his men were starting to give way to the "stubborn" enemy fire. He and one of his lieutenants rushed back to the rear of the company and forbade "any man to move back at the risk of having a sword run through him..." The threat began to work, but the 42nd was starting to fall behind the 2nd Mississippi under Colonel John M. Stone. Soon afterward, Major Feeney of the 42nd caught the attention of Woolard and shouted for the men to continue on ahead: "Then with a shout—such as Southern men otherwise alone can give—we rushed forward..."[12]

Colonel Stone and his men of the 2nd Mississippi continued forward as well in their desperate charge at the enemy line. With the other two regiments falling behind, Stone and his men were exposed to fire at closer ranges than the other regiments. He ordered his men to charge, and shortly thereafter, he fell with a wound. The command of the regiment would now fall to Major John A. Blair.

The left flank of the brigade—the 55th North Carolina under Colonel John K. Connally—now made a desperate push at the enemy's right flank. In the engagement, Connally seized the colors of his regiment and "waved it encouragingly." The display of bravery that Connally showed did not go ignored by his men, nor the enemy, as they continued their advance. Being out front of his men proved to have serious consequences for the brave, young colonel. He was soon shot down after taking up the colors and advancing a short distance. With great haste, Major Belo (of his regiment) went to his side and asked if he had been hurt. "Yes," the colonel replied, "but the litter bearers are here; go on and don't let the Mississippians get ahead of you." The 55th North Carolina proceeded onward through the deadly lead missiles.[13]

The Confederate advance eventually brought the fighting into extremely close quarters, and the casualty toll started rise its ugly figures on both sides. Major Andrew Grover of the 76th New York would be killed while trying to move his men's flank to meet a threat by the 55th North Carolina. The command of the regiment would fall upon Captain John E. Cook, whom General Cutler would praise by saying that "most ably and faithfully did he perform the duty."[14]

The situation was becoming dire in Cutler's front. It was determined that their position could no longer be held, and the order was given by Wadsworth to fall back farther to the rear. Cutler later wrote in his Official Report of the battle: "[The] three regiments under my immediate command fought as only brave men can fight, and held their ground until ordered to fall back ... to the woods on the next ridge."[15]

However, only two of the regiments in front would receive the order—the 76th New York and the 56th Pennsylvania. The 147th New York would meet with destruction when Lieutenant-Colonel Francis C. Miller was wounded in the head at the very moment he received the order and rendered unable to relay the order to his men. The 147th was in the open and taking fire from three sides and had no idea that the order to retreat had been given.

It is difficult for people of this generation to fully comprehend why the 147th New York did not just take the initiative to fall back when they saw the other two regiments retreat. There are three main reasons of why they did not and instead chose to remain and fight it out as long as possible. First, in the dense smoke and loud firing, commanders could barely be seen, let alone heard. It may be possible that the men on the right flank of the 147th did not realize that the 56th Pennsylvania had fallen back. In addition, when the enemy is in your front, it is not hard to imagine trying to stay absolutely focused on the enemy. With the threat of being hit at any moment, your focus is on your rifle, your comrades, and maintaining the line in good order. Lastly, it was not uncommon for a brigade to fall back *en echelon*, just as the attack came near the Herbst Woods, to another position. Therefore, they would have to hold their ground in order to allow a clean getaway for the other regiments.

Eventually, General Wadsworth had enough; he called upon Captain T. E. Ellsworth to get the 147th New York out of their paroles stand. Lieutenant J. V. Pierce recalled the moment that he "discovered the colors of the 56th and 76th N.Y. away back to the rear in the edge of the woods." He also stated: "At the same moment I noticed Hall's Battery limber up, and dash down the Chambersburg Pike…"[16]

Another soldier of the 147th remembered when Hall's Battery retreated, saying that "the battery disappeared in a cloud of dust on the Chambersburg Pike." Much to the dismay of the Federal troops, the battery they had fought dearly to protect was now in full retreat. While the men were witnessing Hall's retreat on their left, the right had opened up again, when a cry came down their line: "They are flanking us on the right." Major Harney, who now commanded the 147th, ordered the companies on the right to be "swung back on the south side of the rail fence…" The maneuver alleviated the pressure that was being felt on the right, but the companies on the left still had to contend with the Confederates popping their heads up over the railroad cut and taking deadly aim at them. Lieutenant J. Volley Pierce of Company "G" went on to describe the contest: "The fight was again fierce and hot; the boys on the right were falling like autumn leaves; the air was full of lead. Men fell all along the line."[17]

The fighting had been continuously surging all around the 147th New York, essentially placing them on an island in the middle of a sea of Confederates tide. Death walked among the troops of both sides as men were being cut to pieces by enemy projectiles. Lieutenant Pierce went on to describe the scene: "The smoke of carnage rose as an incense, and wrapped the folds of the flag defended within its shortened lines. Not a man flinched; none left the field except the wounded; the untouched living and the dead remained." The 147th fought against outstanding odds: the 55th North Carolina began to cause massive pressure on the companies on the right, pressing the flank of the 147th so hard that the defenders gave way, allowing their foes to cross the rail fence that they were defending to the south in an effort to swing around their rear. However, the 147th remained steadfast and, fortunately, Ellsworth soon gave the order to Harney to retreat.[18]

Without delay, Harney yelled at the top of his voice, "In retreat, march!" The order was not exactly military protocol, but it nonetheless worked. The 147th New York now had the order they had desperately sought, and they began to fall back to the rear to join the rest of Cutler's Brigade.

Lieutenant J. V. Pierce and Sergeant Shuttz were in the middle of the retreat and relatively close to one another, when they found a fellow soldier, Private Edwin Aylesworth, lying mortally wounded. Aylesworth begged his two comrades not to leave him behind, but the Rebels were closing fast and soon they would be on their heels and likely captured. Hastily, the two men grabbed the wounded private and hoisted him to his feet. They had only carried him a short way before they reluctantly decided to set him down and retreat on their own. Lieutenant Pierce remembered the facial expression and the words of the young private, who pleaded, "Don't leave me, boys!" After a short time, Aylesworth would die alone in the field, like so many others. Sergeant Shuttz would also be killed that day near Oak Hill.

The retreat was made with such haste that large amounts of Federals simply fled into the railroad cut. Here, a new line was forming and, according to Confederate General Davis, "the enemy made a stubborn resistance…" as they took shots outside the cut and at their pursuers. Soon, however, the 147th would become trapped by the high walls and advancing tides of enemies would overthrow their protected position in the cut.[19]

During this stand, one body of Confederate troops marched through the cut and set up rails to fire from behind: "they saluted us with all their guns, and each one loaded with a bullet." The fire became hot and deadly. The men of the 147th began to seek a way to retreat, and found it by exiting through the south side of the railroad cut, fleeing towards the town to escape. It was here that Sergeant William Wyburn, who was the bearer of the regimental flag, was felled by an enemy bullet. Lieutenant Pierce was there in an instant; supposing the sergeant for dead, he attempted to save the flag, but when he "tried to remove the colors, [Wyburn] held to them with true Irish grit." The desperate Lieutenant ordered him to let them go, but the Irishman looked directly into the face of Pierce and said, "Hold on, I will be up in a minute." The sergeant rolled over, made his way to his feet, and carried the colors the rest of the way.[20]

While the remaining men from the 147th New York continued their way back towards the slopes of Seminary Ridge, which mimicked a shell of its former self, Second Lieutenant Sandy Cook stated that his regiment was now "but a company in size." The men were reforming on the ridge when General Cutler came riding up to Captain Harney and exclaimed, "You have lost your colors, sir." Harney looked back across the field, pointed, and replied "General, the 147th never loses its colors." At that very moment, Wyburn was seen limping across the field, still bleeding from his wound, gallantly carrying their colors. The general presented a lifted spirit when he said, "Boys, I'll take it all back. It is just like cock-fighting today. We fight a little and run a little. There are no supports."[21]

The losses among these three Federal regiments were fearful. The men of the 147th New York brought 380 men into battle on July 1, and their losses were two officers killed and ten wounded and forty-two men killed and 153 wounded—a total loss of 207. The losses of the 56th Pennsylvania had not fared much better; they brought 252 men into battle on July 1 and lost six officers wounded (one mortally) along with eight men killed and sixty-four wounded. The 76th New York brought 407 men into battle on July 1 and lost two officers killed and sixteen wounded, with twenty-seven men killed and 124 wounded.[22]

Captain James A. Hall's 2nd Maine Battery did not fare well in losses either. The battery, which was posted to the left of the 147th New York and across the Railroad Cut, fell back after it too began to take casualties when a small group of Confederates ran along the railroad cut. They crept along, rose to the top, and violently opened a firestorm of musketry on the battery. Hall's men opened up with double canister at the Confederates and then the 147's left (Companies "C" and "G") opened fire on them as well, forcing the Confederate troops back into the unfinished railroad cut and allowing the artillery to keep up their steady fire to their front. Hall remembered: "When, just at this moment, to my surprise I saw my support falling back without any order having been given me to retire." Hall's guns were now left in the open in an advanced position to fend off the enemy for themselves. The 2nd Maine Battery had already lost one gun, with its crew and all its horses shot down. Hall decided that the matter became too great for him and, without orders, he had his men fall back one gun at a time.[23]

Roughly 75 yards in the rear, the right section of guns that had been placed there by Hall to cover their retreat was attacked by charging enemy skirmishers. All the horses were shot down, and the men were forced to finish retiring the guns to the rear by hand.

The battery had been coming off the field splendidly despite the hazardous circumstances that they faced. The last gun was moving to the rear in great style, and it looked as though Hall's Battery would escape the melee almost entirely intact, when luck finally ran out. As the artillery crew was wheeling the last gun to the rear, a Confederate force got close enough to mow down all the horses, and the men had to abandon the piece. Hall, showing great disgust at the thought of losing one of his guns, started to head for the gun to recapture it by himself.

Seeing Hall's movements to recapture the piece, General Wadsworth stopped him; according to Hall, Wadsworth told him "to lose no time, but get [his] battery in position near the town, on the heights, to cover the retiring of the troops." Hall quickly returned to his command to oversee the safe withdrawal of his battery but not before he sent a sergeant and a few other men to try to recover the abandoned artillery piece. The final effort proved to be fruitless and all the men were either killed, wounded, or captured.[24]

After falling back into the position that was desired by Wadsworth, a staff officer of Wadsworth's rode up to Hall and ordered him back to that position. The order was promptly obeyed by the captain, but when the position that was desired had been reached on Seminary Hill, one of Wadsworth's aides ordered him to a new position. On the way to this new position, however, he was fired upon by enemy skirmishers and returned to his assigned position on Seminary Ridge near the Lutheran Theological Seminary. After these confusing movements, Hall then sought out Colonel Wainwright, his chief of artillery, who allowed him to recover the abandoned gun still placed in their front.

After the first day's fighting, Hall's 2nd Maine Battery lost eighteen men killed or wounded and four captured, with twenty-eight horses killed and six wounded. He also lost one gun, with two others suffering broken axles. His crew managed to fire 635 rounds during the entire three-day contest, with most of the action occurring on July 1.

After the retreat of Hall's Battery, a complete Confederate victory appeared a certainty. The Confederate successes thus far had come with a price for the Rebels. As they pursued their fleeing foe, General Davis's regiments became intermixed and commands intertwined. General Davis realized that he was beginning to lose control of his men. In addition, he reported that "many officers and men [had] been killed or wounded, and all much exhausted by the excessive heat..." It seemed as though exhaustion would be the ultimate victory of the day.[25]

Further to the south, the commander of the Union Second Corps, General Winfield Scott Hancock, reported to Meade in person. Hancock, whose troops had marched into Taneytown, Maryland, about a half hour before, had immediately begun to seek further orders. General Meade, who was always straightforward with his corps commanders, began to discuss his plans to Hancock and to get his opinion. Meade asserted that Pipe Creek should be their line of defense since it would provide ground of their own choosing to fight upon and they would be able to gain control of the nearby heights immediately. Hancock remembered: "He said he had made up his mind to fight a battle on what was known as Pipe Creek even though he had not seen the ground. He was judging from the map. It presented more favorable features than any other position that he could see…" Hancock said that Meade had his engineers examine the ground and that "he was then preparing an order for that movement."[26]

Unbeknown to Welles, General Meade would hang desperately onto his Pipe Creek defensive battle plan. Had Meade known about the lay of the land at the town of Gettysburg, it may be likely that Meade would have reconsidered his course of action sooner than he ultimately did.

It was about 11.20 a.m. when Captain Stephen Weld, who had earlier been sent to Meade with a report from Reynolds, rode up to the generals. It was reported that the Confederate Army began to march "a little earlier than was anticipated. Therefore, when General Reynolds attempted to move up from a point … where he had been directed to move that morning, it became a race between him and the enemy which should first get to Gettysburg."[27]

Weld told of the enemy coming in full force and that Reynolds was determined to hold the position until the rest of the army could arrive and take possession of the high ground. General Meade exclaimed, "Good! That is just like Reynolds." After a further explanation of events taking place, Meade said, "Good God! If the enemy get Gettysburg, I am lost."[28]

Upon hearing the news from Weld, the Pipe Creek battle plan was immediately into jeopardy. Meade's nerves, like Lee's for Stuart, came to a boiling point on this hot summer day. Weld remembered that Meade "roundly damned the Chief of Staff … for his slowness in getting out orders." He also went on to explain that he had been working on the Pipe Creek battle plan for "two or three days… and it had taken so long to get the orders out that now it was all useless."[29]

Meade now began to make preparations to try to at least slow the advance of Confederate troops towards Gettysburg. He messaged General Darius Couch: "Can you throw a force in Ewell's rear to threaten him, and at the same time keep your line of retreat open?" The affirmation was given and General Couch did so. He engaged Jenkin's Cavalry and was quickly repulsed. The tide was beginning to turn for the Federal Army as General Couch messaged Halleck: "It [the engaged force] has been attacked by a body of cavalry at least and just now things do not look well."[30]

Soon thereafter, Weld began to ride back towards Gettysburg to return to General Reynolds. Halfway back, he was met by an orderly who told him that Reynolds was shot. "I did not believe him," Weld explained, "but of course felt very anxious, and rode on as fast as possible to ascertain the truth of the matter.… I met Captain Mitchell with an ambulance, and General Reynolds's body. I felt very badly indeed about his death, as he had always treated me very kindly." Weld went on to describe Reynolds: "Brave, kind-hearted, modest, somewhat rough and wanting polish, he was a type of the true soldier. I cannot realize that he is dead ... and now to think of him as dead seems an impossibility."[31]

It was not long after Captain Weld set off to return to his officer that General Meade also received word that General Reynolds was either killed or wounded and that General Howard was now in command of the Federal Troops on the battlefield. The time was about 1.10 p.m. and General Hancock was again summoned by General Meade to his headquarters. Lieutenant Colonel Charles Morgan of Hancock's staff remembered: "Generals Meade and Butterfield were both present. It was not then known whether General Reynolds was dead or not, and General Hancock's order was conditional, to assume command only in case General Reynolds was wounded." However, General Meade was notified that General Howard was the senior commander on the battlefield even when Hancock arrived. To this, General Meade responded stating that he "could not help it; that he knew General Hancock, but did not know General Howard so well, and at this crisis he must have a man he knew and could trust." General Meade told Hancock: "If you consider the ground and position there a better one to fight a battle, under existing circumstances, you will advise the general, and he will order all the troops up."[32]

Before he too set off, General Hancock put General John Gibbon in charge of the Second Corps. Like Hancock, Gibbon was not the next senior officer in line, but General Meade made the recommendation because he felt Gibbon was the most suitable person for it. General Hancock traveled to Gettysburg in an ambulance in order to be able to study his maps. General Meade still held on to his Pipe Creek plan, but chances for its implementation dimmed with each passing minute. The final decision was still left to General Hancock to ascertain whether it would be worth moving the entire Army of the Potomac to Gettysburg to establish a defensive position there.

About 4 miles from Gettysburg, an ambulance coming from the town was seen by General Hancock and his small party of officers. It was then that General Hancock learned that the body of his good friend General John Reynold's was inside. Silence set in among the shocked men as they continued on to Gettysburg.

Meanwhile, still in reserve on Seminary Ridge, Colonel Rufus Dawes and his 6th Wisconsin regiment awaited further orders. They were in position to witness the action on both sides of the road and realized that they would soon be needed. Colonel Dawes anxiously awaited the command to advance and march his troops to their date with destiny.

5

The First Corps Strikes Back

About this time on the Seminary Ridge, Colonel Rufus Dawes and his 6th Wisconsin troops awaited orders. As Cutler's troops began to stream back through the fields and woods towards the rear, the order finally came. Lieutenant Meredith Jones of General Doubleday's staff came at a gallop to Dawes and said, "General Doubleday directs that you move your regiment at once to the right." Dawes had begun making preparations to obey the order when the brigade adjutant, Captain James. D. Wood, rode up and spoke about the seriousness of the order and said that the "Rebels were driving Cutler's men." Colonel Dawes moved his men on a run toward the fighting near the unfinished railroad cut.

Dawes led his men forward and, as they approached the Confederate tide, he witnessed the last of Cutler's men falling back along with the withdrawal of Hall's Battery. Dawes ordered his men into line of battle once they approached the Chambersburg Pike and began to encounter the enemy. As the order was being fulfilled, Dawes' horse took a hard plunge to the ground after been wounded in the breast. The worried men of the 6th Wisconsin looked on nervously, but Dawes was unharmed and quickly jumped to his feet, accompanied by a hearty cheer from his boys. For the rest of the battle, Dawes fought on foot.

The men continued to advance in line of battle until they reached a narrow fence that ran along the Pike. Using the rails to steady their rifles, Dawes promptly gave the order, "Fire by file." Dawes described the scene: "In the field beyond the turnpike, a long line of Confederates could be seen running forward and firing." The men of the 6th Wisconsin kept up their fire and checked the advancement of Davis's Brigade on Cutler's fleeing forces. Joe Davis described this as being engaged by a force that was "renewed ... and ... greatly superior numbers." While Dawes remembered that the Confederate line "swayed and bent, and suddenly stopped firing and the men ran into the railroad cut."

With the enemy now pouring a deadly effective fire from a strong defensive position, Dawes pondered his options, but only for a moment

Rufus Dawes.
(*Photo courtesy of Library of Congress*)

until he noticed that he had help. The men of the 95th New York Infantry and the 14th Brooklyn fell in on the left of his regiment. Dawes ran over to Major Edward Pye, now commander of the 95th New York after Colonel George H. Biddle was wounded, and said, "We must charge." The major quickly replied, "Charge it is." A moment later, Dawes yelled at the top of his voice the command and his men jumped up and over the fence and charged their enemies still in the cut. Along with many others, Captain John Ticknor never made it over the fence. He fell dead in the midst of his climb.

The three Federal regiments stormed across the field and directly towards the trapped Rebels. Dawes recalled: "We were receiving a fearfully destructive fire from the hidden enemy. Men who had been shot were leaving the ranks in crowds." The devastating enemy fire, which Dawes spoke of, would cost him nearly one man for every yard gained over the deadly field of fire.

Dawes kept his men moving forward, however, and kept giving the order, "Align on the colors! Close up on the colors! Close up on the colors!" Dawes watched as the colors of the regiment fell several times, yet each time they fell, another man was there to pick it up, hoist it in the air among the flying lead, and keep proceeding forward towards the crest of the railroad cut.[1]

The colors of the 2nd Mississippi were seen also seen fluttering above the crest. Confederate color bearer W. B. Murphy, of the 2nd Mississippi, recalled:

> My color guards were all killed and wounded in less than five minutes ... also my colors were shot more than one dozen times, and the flag staff was hit and splintered two or three times. Just at that time a squad of soldiers made a rush for my colors.... They were all killed or wounded.... They still kept rushing for my flag.... Over a dozen men fell killed or wounded, and then a large man made a rush for me and the flag. As I tore the flag from the staff, he took hold of me and the color.[2]

The large man was Corporal Frank Waller of the 6th Wisconsin, who would receive the Congressional Medal of Honor for his deeds done this day and the capture of the 2nd Mississippi's flag.

During one of the attempts for the 2nd Mississippi flag, Corporal Lewis W. Eggleston of the 6th Wisconsin was mortally wounded when he sprang forward in the attempt to seize the colors. Private David Anderson, known as "Rocky Mountain Anderson," was nearby and witnessed the slaying of the young corporal. He immediately became enraged and sought out the Confederate who pulled the trigger. Once he located him, Anderson "swung aloft his musket and with a terrific blow split the skull of the Rebel who had shot young Eggleston."[3]

The remaining men of the 6th Wisconsin shouted: "Throw down your muskets! Down with your muskets!" Dawes made a mad rush to the very crest of the cut and, along with Adjutant Edward Brooks and about twenty men, got into position to fire down the length of the cut. The bewildered Confederates looked up at Dawes and his remaining men with utter shock and disbelief. "Where is the colonel of this regiment?" demanded Dawes. Major John Blair shouted, "Who are you?" Dawes informed him, "I command this regiment. Surrender, or I will fire." The officer calmly surrendered his sword to him, and the men remaining in the cut threw down their muskets. Dawes was soon left holding a large bundle of swords from other officers who followed suit.

Dawes was astonished at the discipline of his men when they made the charge into the railroad cut. He later described his pride in his men:

> The coolness, self-possession, and discipline which held back our men from pouring in a general volley saved a hundred lives of the enemy, and as my mind goes back to the fearful excitement of the moment, I marvel at it.[4]

Dawes' men would suffer 168 casualties out of 420 men during their short fight on July 1. Every man of the color guard was either killed, missing, or wounded. Dawes later wrote to his fiancée on July 6 of the horrors that inflicted him from the conflict: "The experience of the past few days seem more like a horrible dream than the reality.... Our bravest and best are cold in the ground or suffering on beds." Later in the letter, he went on to describe the sufferings at the railroad cut of one soldier named Corporal James Kelly. The young corporal had been shot through the breast and "came staggering up to [Dawes] before he fell and, opening his shirt to show the wound, said 'Colonel, won't you write to my folks that I died a soldier.'"[5]

Dawes never quite recovered over the loss of so many of his men that day. It was this loss that would later derail Dawes into a condition known today as post-traumatic stress disorder (P.T.S.D.).

Soon after much of Davis's Brigade had surrendered, Dawes instructed Major John Hauser to lead the prisoners away. Upon peering out into the field, the men of the 6th Wisconsin noticed Hall's single abandoned gun. Knowing that the gun could not simply be left in the hands of the enemy, Captain Rollin P. Converse took charge of the matter and began to withdraw the artillery piece until he reached the Chambersburg Pike, where he relinquished the gun to the rightful owner (Hall) and made his way to the rear.

The 95th New York also suffered greatly during the fighting. They brought 261 men into the fray that morning and lost 115 to enemy bullets in the half hour they were engaged. To their left, the 14th Brooklyn (known as the "Red-Legged Devils"), under Colonel Edward Fowler, brought 356 men into battle on July 1 and suffered roughly 220 casualties after the three days of fighting. They would be one of the few regiments to have fought on all three days of battle.[6]

A temporary lull in the fighting began to take place around noon as General Davis attempted to reorganize his men. The early morning's fighting had finally been enough for General Heth, who had disobeyed direct orders by General Lee not to bring on a general engagement with the enemy. Heth later made an excuse for his actions in his Official Report: "Archer and Davis were now directed to advance, the object being to feel the enemy; to make a forced reconnaissance, and determine in what force the enemy were." Heth had also been warned several times by a few of his brigade commanders (Archer included) that the enemy strength was still unknown. Now, Heth had lost a heavy amount of men, and much of that loss could be directly attributed to him and his decisions.[7]

The lull in the fighting lasted about two hours and General Doubleday made good time of it. He shifted the troops of the Iron Brigade around to be better aligned for an attack (from left to right: 19th Indiana, 24th Michigan, 7th Wisconsin, and the 2nd Wisconsin). The divisions of General Thomas A. Rowley and General John Robinson, which roughly numbered 6,000 men, also arrived during the lull. General Doubleday personally directed the placement of those troops. In Rowley's Division, he placed Chapman Biddle's Brigade, consisting of the 121st Pennsylvania, 80th New York, 142nd Pennsylvania, and the 151st Pennsylvania (which was held in reserve), to the left of Morrow's Brigade—which remained in Herbst Woods.

Doubleday then placed Colonel Roy Stone's "Bucktail Brigade" on the right of Morrow's Brigade. Their nickname deviated from the characteristic that they pinned buck tails on to the tops of their kepis, which gave the brigade its own distinction. Stone's regiments filed in front of the McPherson barn and consisted of the 143rd, 149th, and the 150th Pennsylvania Infantry Regiments.

General Robinson's division was posted near the Seminary and threw up breastworks to block any advance of enemy troops in their front in the event the rest of the First Corps being pushed back. Although they were initially placed in reserve, before long, Robinson's men would be hotly engaged with troops from a number of different Confederate brigades.

Henry Baxter. (*Photo courtesy of Library of Congress*)

The only brigade of Robinson's Division ordered to move forward and placed in the line of battle at this time was that of forty-two-year-old General Henry Baxter. The regiments of his brigade were made of the 12th Massachusetts, the 83rd and 97th New York, and the 11th, 88th, and 90th Pennsylvania Infantry Regiments, all of which were placed to the immediate right of Cutler's Brigade.

As for Robinson's Second Brigade, which was commanded by fifty-year-old General Gabriel Paul, it remained in support of Baxter's men and off the line for right now. The Second Brigade consisted of the 16th Maine, 13th Massachusetts, 94th New York, and 107th Pennsylvania Infantry Regiments.[8]

As the lull progressed, both sides took this time to refill canteens and ammo boxes. Many of the dead and wounded still remained where they had fallen, while a very few were being sent to receive proper medical attention. The fighting had been severe thus far, and the Federals still held the field despite being pushed back by Davis's troops. However, reinforcements were on the way for the Confederates, and a brand-new counterattack would soon take place.

Before that, a new general would take overall command of the battlefield—General Oliver O. Howard, commander of the Eleventh Corps. Howard received orders from General Meade around 3.30 a.m. on July 1 to move the Eleventh Corps to within supporting distance of the First Corps. Once the Eleventh Corps made it to within 2 miles of town, Reynolds sent Howard orders detailing where to place his troops.

The sound of battle caught the attention of General Howard, and he soon set off in order to locate General Reynolds to report to him in person upon arriving on the battlefield. When one of Reynolds' aides met Howard near a peach orchard, Howard asked him where he should position his troops. The aide replied, "Stop anywhere about here, according to your judgment, at present."[9]

This presented a problem in Howard's mind. He was in no location to deploy his men with any cover, and his current location was certainly not high ground. Before the firing began again, to the west of town, Howard dispatched Captain Daniel Hall to find Reynolds. In the meantime, Howard began to seek a satisfactory place to deploy his men: "Not finding a point from which I could get an extended view and noticing higher ground eastward, I … rode to the highest point of the Cemetery Ridge."[10]

The view that befell the general's eyes on Cemetery Hill was stunning. It was a commanding view of the terrain west and south of town and Cemetery Hill was a good place to fall back to if the need arose. Howard turned to Colonel T. A. Meysenberg, who was serving as Howard's Assistant Adjutant General, and said, "This seems to be a good position,

Colonel." The colonel agreeably stated back, "It is the only position, General." General Howard unwittingly stumbled onto what would be a key element during the entire Battle of Gettysburg. Here, he would set up his headquarters at the gatehouse and prepare his troops to make a stand farther to the front of his position.[11]

Cemetery Hill, however, had a drawback. Howard could not see the formations of the troops fighting northwest of town from his current position, and he soon rode into town and established a better observation post on the roof of the Fahnestock Dry Goods Store just south of the town square.

Once at the top, General Howard then had the commanding view of the battle on McPherson Ridge that he desperately needed. Upon peering from his elevated position, he noticed General Buford's cavalry troops who remained on the flanks of the First Corps and also saw the wounded and prisoners being escorted to the rear. As Howard looked upon the lanes and roads around the town, he saw a young soldier riding up the street below. Stopping below the general, he peered up, saluted General Howard, and said, "General Reynolds is wounded, sir." Shocked, Howard replied, "I am very sorry; I hope he will be able to keep the field." Howard would later write in his Official Report that, when he learned of Reynolds being wounded, "[he at first] hoped his wound might be slight, and that he would continue to command."[12]

Howard and the other officers of his staff knew that it was extremely costly to lose such a highly regarded, experienced general such as John Reynolds. While still on the roof of the building, another staff officer soon came riding up. It was none other than Major William Riddle, who belonged with Reynolds' staff. He stated to Howard, "General Reynolds is dead, and you are the senior officer on the field." Howard immediately knew this put him in command of the left wing of the Army of the Potomac and placed General Carl Schurz to take over command of the Eleventh Corps. The general gathered his thoughts and stated: "God helping us, we will stay here till the army comes."[13]

After falling back, General Buford reestablished his line on the flanks of the First Corps and Eleventh Corps. On the road north of town, some of his men encountered enemy troops of General Jubal Early's Division. This was immediately reported to General Howard, who decided to move both General Francis Barlow's First Division and General Carl Schurz's Third Division (now being commanded by General Alexander Schimmelfennig) up to the ridge and plain north of town to protect against any attack from that direction.

The Eleventh Corps hurried through town and began to deploy into a line of battle, with Schimmelfennig's troops placed on the flank right of

The Death of General Reynolds.
(Sketch done by Alfred Waud, courtesy of Library of Congress)

the First Corps. Barlow and Howard rode together out of town to where Schimmelfennig had been positioned and Barlow placed his men on and near a small hill named Blocher's Knoll. General Adolph von Steinwehr's Second Division would be held in reserve for the time being on Cemetery Ridge and along the Baltimore Pike.

General Howard realized the gravity of the situation. He knew that the First Corps had already been heavily engaged by General A. P. Hill's Confederate Third Corps from the west in heavy force. Keeping in mind that he also knew of all the reported enemy troop movements from the day before and was aware that the Confederates had at least another division behind those which the Federal First Corps had already faced, it was likely that his men would soon be engaged in combat with the men of General Richard S. Ewell's Confederate Second Corps. In an attempt to bring up support for the left wing of the First Corps, Howard sent word for General Dan Sickles' Third Corps at Emmitsburg and General Henry Slocum's Twelfth Corps at Two Taverns to come quickly to Gettysburg. As for artillery, Major Thomas Osborn's guns were the first to be posted on Cemetery Hill. While, Hubert Dilger's Ohio Battery and William Wheeler's New York Battery were hurried through the town and placed to the right of the First Corps.

The time was now nearing 2 p.m., and the lull in the fighting had finally came to its conclusion. After becoming situated, Howard began to check out on the First Corps, after which he decided to ride back to Cemetery Hill

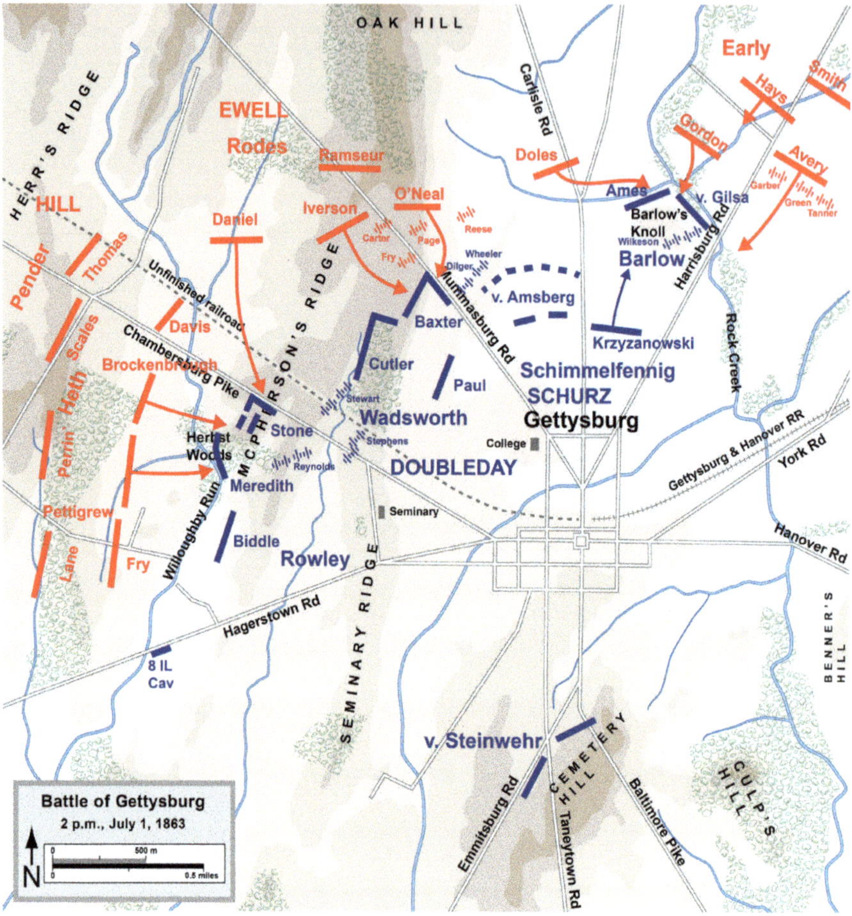

July 1, 2 p.m. (*Map by Hal Jespersen, www.cwmaps.com*)

to further review his line of defense. Captain Stephen Weld, one of General Reynolds' aides, rode up and found General Howard standing in Evergreen Cemetery. A brief discussion was soon taking place when Weld noticed a line of Confederate troops moving down from the north of town from the vicinity of Oak Hill. Weld exclaimed, "General, those are the rebs, why don't you fire at them?" Howard scanned the area with his field glasses and stated, "No, I think they are our men." Weld responded, "They are not, sir, they are the rebs." He asked one of his staff members to view the situation and tell him what they thought of the matter: "General, those are long lines of the enemy!" The Confederates were beginning to renew their attack.

Earlier in the morning, before the Confederate Army became engaged in combat, General Lee woke in his usual cheerful spirits near Greenwood. However, Lee had been without his head cavalry officer, J. E. B. Stuart, now for nearly a week, and Lee's concern was beginning to build due to the lack of intelligence reports from General Stuart or his troops. Nevertheless, General Lee remained jaunty and summoned General Longstreet to ride with him as they proceeded to Cashtown. Longstreet was delighted to be accompanied by the commanding general, and they both rode until reaching General Edward Johnson of Ewell's Third Corps along the pike. General Johnson had kept his command back from the rest of the Third Corps to escort Ewell's trains. The road towards Cashtown was blocked by wagons, horses, and men. At this point, Lee ordered Longstreet's command to halt in order to allow Johnson's Division to catch up with the rest of the Third Corps—a blunder that he would soon regret as Longstreet's First Corps would be left waiting for several hours and it would take until nearly dark before they reached Gettysburg.[14]

Soon, the stationary generals heard cannon fire off in the distance. Both officers sat on their horses and tried to determine where, and by whom, it was coming from. They quickly surmised that it was beyond Cashtown, but the source was unknown since there were two different infantry corps in front of Longstreet's. After a few minutes, the firing abruptly increased and Lee allowed Longstreet's troops to resume their wait; the two officers then set off to determine where the firing was coming from and to meet up with General A. P. Hill, commanding the Third Corps, at Cashtown.

There, General Hill, who had been ill, had just gotten out of bed when General Lee and General Longstreet arrived. Hill had also heard the cannon fire taking place and was also concerned about it since Hill's orders to one of division commanders, Henry Heth, had been to only make a reconnaissance into the area around and in the town of Gettysburg.

The generals spoke briefly—a reconnaissance had indeed been done a day earlier by troops of General James Pettigrew's Division of Hill's Third Corps and did encounter enemy troops before Pettigrew's men withdrew. Hill was now attempting to determine the size of the enemy force ahead by sending Heth's Division forward to Gettysburg. He also explained to Heth that "if he found infantry opposed to him, to report the fact immediately, without forcing an engagement."[15]

General Lee was becoming very anxious about not having General J. E. B. Stuart at his disposal to ascertain the whereabouts of the enemy and the size of the force. In recent years, Stuart time and time again proved himself a worthy and obedient soldier and leader. This time, however, it was different. Lee could feel the pressure of being led into a battle blind. Colonel Walter Taylor, one of General Lee's aides, had written about the importance of cavalry:

> An army without cavalry in a strange and hostile country is as a man deprived of his eyesight and beset by enemies; he may be never

> so brace and strong, but he cannot intelligently administer a single effective below.[16]

While remaining in the rear and allowing Hill to go to the front to ascertain the condition of his troops, General Lee summoned General Richard H. Anderson, a division commander in Hill's III Corps. Anderson remembered that "[he] found General Lee intently listening to the fire of the guns, and very much disturbed and depressed." The commanding general's mood was certainly becoming foul at this point, as noted by Anderson: "I cannot think what has become of Stuart. I ought to have heard from him long before now. He may have met with disaster, but I hope not. In the absence of reports from him, I am in ignorance as to what we have in front of us here. It may be the whole Federal Army, or it may be only a detachment." Suddenly Lee made a bold statement about the possibility of the upcoming conflict: "If it is the whole Federal force, we must fight a battle here. If we do not gain a victory, those defiles and gorges which we passed this morning will shelter us from disaster." Soon after making these few statements, General Lee ordered General Anderson and his troops to move forward towards the emitting sound of battle.[17]

Soon thereafter, Major Campbell Brown of Ewell's Second Corps delivered a message to General Lee about the movements of that corps. Earlier in the day, General Ewell had received notice that General A. P. Hill's troops were moving toward the town of Gettysburg in the morning. This prompted General Ewell to move his troops toward the towns of Cashtown and Gettysburg as well. Major Brown reported this fact to General Lee, which did not help Lee's mood. He had troops moving toward the sound of battle instead of reporting to General Lee for orders first, further casting the situation out from Lee's grasp.

The situation was getting out of hand for General Lee, who was beginning to feel as though he had lost command and control of his army. Major Brown recorded: "With a peculiar searching, almost querulous, impatience, which I had never seen in him before (had asked) whether Gen'l Ewell had heard anything from Gen'l Jeb Stuart, and on my replying in the negative, said that he had heard nothing from or of him for three days, and that Gen'l Stuart had not complied with his instructions.... I see by a paper that he is near Washington." General Lee stated: "A scout reports Meade's whole army marching this way, but that is all I know about his position." General Lee told Major Brown to report back to General Ewell with instructions to send out his left and try to open communications with General Stuart.[18]

Major Brown never saw this attitude in the commanding general before, which came across as a surprise by the sudden outburst displayed be Lee. Brown later admitted: "I now appreciate that he was really uneasy and irritated by Stuart's conduct and had no objection to his hearing of it.... As I left Gen'l Lee to return by the way I had come, Gen'l Lee started on toward Hill's front." It was clear to Major Brown—and most of the people around General Lee that morning—that Lee's first priority appeared to be locating General Stuart. Lee still had no idea that the Union First Corps was already on the battlefield, that the Eleventh Corps was just arriving, and that two other corps had been summoned by the opposing force.[19]

General Meade was a little more fortunate than General Lee on the morning of July 1. He had received several reports pertaining to the enemy's whereabouts and the direction in which they were heading. Meade reported on July 1 to General-in-Chief Henry Halleck in Washington, D.C., of his knowledge of the troops in the area: "Ewell is marching at Heidelberg; A. P. Hill is massed behind the mountains at Cashtown; Longstreet somewhere between Chambersburg and the mountains." Meade went on to report that he would "not advance any, but prepare to receive an attack in case Lee makes one."[20]

General Meade had a different outlook on the impending battle. Whereas General Lee approached with a more aggressive frame of mind, Meade

John Buford.
(Photo courtesy of Library of Congress)

had a strict defensive mindset. He dispatched General Halleck about noon on July 1: "I am looking to the protection of Washington and fighting my army to the best advantage." With this dispatch, General Meade made his goals clear: he would protect the main cities while straining every nerve of the Confederate Army possible.[21]

Meade would also receive a vote of confidence from Secretary of the Navy Gideon Welles, who took careful notice to the caution in the orders given to Meade: "Lee and his army are well advanced into Pennsylvania.... Halleck is bent on driving them back, not on intercepting their retreat; is full of zeal to drive them out of Pennsylvania." Welles then expressed his own confidence in Meade: "Meade will, I trust, keep closer to them than some others have done."[22]

The situation was becoming drastic for the Federal Army and General Meade felt as though he was losing control. This feeling was becoming prevalent throughout the outgunned Federal force as well. Generals like Buford grumbled to their commander, General Pleasonton: "The enemy's line is a semicircle on the height from north to west. General Reynolds was killed early this morning. In my opinion there seems to be no directing person." Buford went on to close his letter by saying, "We need help now."[23]

6

"Some Grand Panorama..."

Although General John Buford may not have known it at that moment, help was on the field. The Eleventh Corps began to assume positions north of town in support the right flank of the First Corps. General Dan Sickles was also now moving his Third Corps at a steady pace towards Gettysburg, and the men of the Twelfth Corps, under the command of General Henry Slocum, were also within a short distance of the battlefield at Gettysburg. Captain Julian Hinkley of the 3rd Wisconsin Infantry Regiment, in the Twelfth Corps, wrote about being so close to the sounds of the fighting on July 1:

> At noon ... while we were preparing our dinner at Two Taverns ... the distant rumbling of artillery to the north announced to us the opening of a great battle. The cannonading became more and more furious as the minutes passed until in the distance it sounded like one continual roll of thunder.[1]

Regretfully, Slocum would refuse to move his men toward Gettysburg until later that day—too late to make any difference on the outcome of the fighting on July 1. Howard had to settle for knowing that the flank of the First Corps was being protected by the only corps available, the Eleventh Corps.

Earlier, to the north of town and just before the lull commenced, General Robert Rodes' Division of General Ewell's Second Corps were in the process of marching toward Cashtown via the Carlisle Road. Upon learning that General A. P. Hill's Third Corps would be pressing east from Cashtown towards Gettysburg, General Ewell directed his entire corps to follow suit. When the troops under Rodes' command were within 4 miles of Gettysburg, they began to hear gunfire in their front. General Ewell marched ahead of General George P. Doles' Brigade. They noticed the slackened pace of the men that followed and ordered up the brass band of the 4th Georgia Infantry Regiment to play for them. As one soldier remembered: "The music had a most exhilarating effect, and off the men marched, inspired by the

"The Opening Gun." (*Photo courtesy of Katie Campbell*)

presence of the generals and the strains of the 'Tom, March on' by the band. I never saw anything so magical in its effect."[2]

As they drew nearer to the town of Gettysburg, General Rodes began to make the necessary preparations to perform an immediate attack if one was so deemed necessary. Rodes rushed a small group of officers towards an opening in the woods near Oak Ridge in front of them. Upon breaking the woods line, the view that beseeched the officers took their breaths away. Rodes recognized that it was Chancellorsville all over again:

> On arriving on the field, I found … I could strike the force of the enemy with which General Hill's troops were engaged upon the flank … and that, besides moving under cover, whenever we struck the enemy we could engage him with the advantage in ground.[3]

It was by sheer chance that he arrived in such a position. For the time being, at least, the enemy's right flank was exposed and could easily be turned. This would create an opportunity for Hill's Corps to finish the job they started on the southern end of the battlefield and collapse the entire Federal First Corps in on itself.

Rodes quickly sent word back to his brigade commanders and moved his division up and deployed them along the summit of Oak Ridge. Private James Thompson of the 6th Alabama Infantry Regiment gasped at the sight, remembering that "this was the only time during the war that [they] were in position to get such a view of contending forces. It seemed like some grand panorama with the sounds of conflict added."[4]

General Rodes' Divison was composed of veterans from several southern states in its five brigades. The brigade commanders were Generals Stephen D. Ramseur (2nd, 4th, 14th, and 30th North Carolina Infantry Regiments), General George P. Doles (4th, 12th, 21st, and 44th Georgia Infantry Regiments), General Alfred Iverson (5th, 12th, 20th, and 23rd North Carolina Infantry Regiments), General Junius Daniel (2nd North Carolina Infantry Battalion, 32nd, 43rd, 45th, and 53rd Infantry Regiments), and Colonel Edward O'Neal (3rd, 5th, 6th, and 26th Alabama Infantry Regiments).

On the Federal side, General Henry Baxter (First Corps, Second Division, Second Brigade) received orders to "send forward two regiments at once." He chose the 11th Pennsylvania Infantry Regiment and the 97th New York Infantry Regiment, forming them into a line of battle to the right of General Wadsworth's Division, which gave strength and stability to Wadsworth's already battered line. The rest of Baxter's Brigade was soon ordered up as well, forming to the right of the rest of the brigade. By the time these maneuvers were completed, Baxter's line of battle extended to the Mummasburg Road, where it angled back and ran parallel to the road a few hundred yards, as "indications being that [they would] be attacked on [their] right flank."[5]

To his surprise, Rodes later admitted that "the enemy began to show large bodies of men in front of the town, most of which were directed upon the position which [he] held.... Either these last troops, or others which had hitherto been unobserved behind the same body of woods, soon made their appearance directly opposite [his] center."[6]

Baxter had the 83rd New York Infantry Regiment to the left and the 88th Pennsylvania Infantry Regiment formed to the right of the 90th Pennsylvania Infantry Regiment and faced toward the sloping ground that General Rodes' troops were beginning to occupy. Rodes knew of General Lee's order to not bring on a general engagement; however, as Colonel Walter Taylor of General Lee's staff later said, "neither side sought or expected a general engagement; and yet, brought thus unexpectedly in the presence of each other, found a conflict unavoidable."[7]

Major Campbell Brown rode up just as General's Ewell and Rodes were beginning to place their guns to attack the enemy in their front. It was their belief that at any moment they would be attacked by those Federal forces and wanted to beat them to the punch. Brown repeated General Lee's orders, but it was too late. Soon after Baxter's Brigade got into position, Lieutenant Colonel Thomas H. Carter's Battalion opened fire, which drew the immediate response of several Federal Batteries.

General Ewell would write in his Official Report: "It was too late to avoid an engagement without abandoning the position already taken up, and I determined to push the attack vigorously." In doing this, Ewell directly disobeyed General Lee's orders just as Heth had earlier. However, the Confederate force was ill-prepared; in their haste to make an attack, General Rodes said "all the troops were in the woods excepting Doles' and a portion ... [O'Neal's] brigades ... but all were subjected to some loss or annoyance from the enemy's artillery." The firing became so annoying that General Rodes ordered O'Neal's Brigade toward Iverson's Brigade, which put the larger part of the Confederate Division near the John Forney house.[8]

Arriving about this time to observe the battle was General Lee, who observed from his position on Belmont Ridge. General Rodes's Brigade was beginning to succumb to heavy enemy artillery fire, when General Heth rode up to General Lee, who had been watching the transpiring events unfolding in front of him. Heth stated: "Rodes is very heavily engaged, had I not better attack?" General Lee's reply was quick and stern: "No, I am not prepared to bring on a general engagement to-day. Longstreet is not up." When Heth returned to his command, he found the enemy becoming massed in his front (Stone's and Biddle's Brigades) and again rode to General Lee to request permission to attack the massed Federals. This time approval was given. General Heth went back to his position and prepared his men to advance.[9]

General Lee's plans were beginning to unravel. He did not want the fight, but the fight wanted him. The military term for the transpiring sequence of events on that July day was a "meeting engagement." The term basically meant that the two armies stumbled into the fight by chance. The reconnaissance done by General Hill's troops in the early morning had inadvertently begun what would become known as the bloodiest battle in the Civil War. Once engaged with nearly 4,000 men, it became almost impossible for General Heth's Division to pull out of the fight when the Federal First Corps arrived on the battlefield.

General Ewell and General Rodes were no better at following General Lee's orders not to bring on a general engagement. They followed the sound of the guns, and soon Rodes would begin to order his brigades forward to attack the enemy. Rodes eventually determined to attack from his position on Oak Ridge. Directing his attack at the right flank and center of the Federal First Corps by simultaneously using O'Neal's and Iverson's Brigades, General Rodes would then strike the Federal center and across the unfinished railroad cut with General Daniels' Brigade and, eventually, General Doles' Brigade. Meanwhile, General Ramseur's Brigade was held in reserve for the time being.[10]

At his position on Oak Hill, one soldier in the 12th North Carolina Infantry regiment remembered Rodes saying: "Boys, they are advancing upon us; go ahead and meet them!" Before long, three brigades moved forward, but confusion among the brigades soon occurred. As General Rodes reported: "The three first-mentioned regiments moved with alacrity (but not in accordance with my orders as to direction) and in confusion into the action."[11]

The cause of this "confusion" could directly be attributed to Colonel O'Neal, who, in his haste, sent his men forward into the fray before Iverson's men were fully ready. O'Neal's men moved off the line so quickly that they left two of their regiments behind and began the attack with only the 6th, 12th, and 26th Alabama Infantry Regiments. When General Rodes saw what was transpiring, he personally ordered the 5th Alabama Infantry Regiment to advance immediately. General Rodes recalled: "To my surprise, in giving this command to its colonel (the 5th), I found that Colonel O'Neal, instead of personally superintending the movements of his brigade, had chosen to remain with his reserve regiment." Now, not only did their timing not match up to the correlated attack plan, their commander stayed behind and advanced his men.[12]

This undoubtedly angered General Rodes, who now personally directed each of his other brigade commanders exactly where to attack. Unfortunately for O'Neal's men, it was too late. They were in the open and attacking weakly without any order or direction. This was almost unheard of in the Army of Northern Virginia, where it was expected that the officers personally direct and lead their men when attacking the enemy.

The Alabamians hit the four Federal brigades refused along the Mummasburg Road that were supported by Captain Hubert Dilger's 1st Ohio Light Artillery. Dilger ordered his six-gun battery to open on the Confederate attackers with double canister.

Huge gaps were created in the long lines of Alabamians due to this destructive fire and men began to fall by the scores. Captain Robert E. Park of the 12th Alabama Infantry Regiment would be one of the men of O'Neal's Brigade who would suffer the terrible effects of the day. As he was advancing over ground that was being shelled by Dilger's artillery, his captain, James T. Davis of Company "D," "was killed near ... and his brains scattered upon [him]. He was a brave, good man." Halfway across the fields, the Alabamians were subject to the unmerciful volleys of lead missiles delivered by their adversaries, which briefly halted their advance.[13]

O'Neal's Brigade had marched themselves right into a firestorm. The shells were crashing, the roar of the musketry was deafening, and the orders of officers were muffled by the constant rattle of battle. Witnessing it all was Iverson's Brigade, who were still in the rear not yet up in support of the attack. The Confederates soon made a grand attempt to overthrow the Federal stronghold by mounting a desperate charge. Captain Park described the charge: "There Lieut. Wright was wounded in the head by my side. I gave him some water from my canteen, and made him lie down close to the ground, as balls were falling thick and fast around us, and whizzing past and often striking someone near."[14]

The Baxter's men had a strong defensive position that allowed them to maintain good alignment for the oncoming enemy. Holes in the line were filled by the next man, while an incessant roar of musketry was delivered by both fronts. Hard, heavy fighting, like what O'Neal's men were experiencing, was an example of where a good leader would come into play. General Baxter, unlike O'Neal, remained in the thick of the fight with his brigade and was able to communicate his orders quickly and effectively. Instead, men like Captain Park continually led his men onward until, halting briefly to realign their ranks, Park too took a ball in his hip. The officer winced in pain as he plowed to the ground. He later stated: "It was a wonder, a miracle, I was not afterward shot a half dozen times."[15]

Soon afterward, the order came through to the Confederate attackers to fall back to a small stone wall running near the Oak Hill incline. This highly sought after order was willingly executed by the deprived Confederate troops, leaving scores behind. Captain Park remained on the ground until a fleeing officer, Captain Nicholson, helped him hobble back, even though Park pleaded with Nicholson to leave him and go to safety himself. O'Neal's command was upset at the incompetence he had displayed; however, the best quality of soldiers remained poised to move at their commander's will. Later, Rodes stated his disgust in his Official Report when he wrote that O'Neal had been "repulsed quickly and with loss."[16]

Meanwhile, General Howard had made a request for help earlier when he asked General Slocum to bring his Twelfth Corps to Gettysburg. It was now about 3.45 p.m. and General Howard's patience, understandably, began to wear thin. General Slocum would again receive word of the fighting taking place in Gettysburg, while General Howard began to feel the heat from his own division commanders, who were asking for reinforcements to support them. He steadfastly reassured them: "Hold out a little longer, if possible; I am expecting General Slocum every moment."[17]

General Slocum, however, still would not adhere to the orders given by Howard, remaining at his position near Two Taverns while General Sickles' Third Corps made haste in their approach about 5 miles away. Eventually, Howard's patience could be tested no more. He had waited long enough and sent Major Charles Howard, his own brother, to seek out Slocum and convince him to come "at once, and send one Division to the right and the other to the left of Gettysburg." Again, Slocum declined to go upon Howard's request, arguing that General Meade, like Lee, did not desire to bring about a full engagement. For now, Slocum would hold his Twelfth Corps at Two Taverns and Howard would be forced to slug it out with the two corps he had already in position and taking causalities.[18]

On Oak Ridge, General Baxter's men got very little rest before Iverson's Brigade of North Carolinians began to attack towards a gap that existed between his and Cutler's lines. The commander of the First Corps, Second Division, General John C. Robinson, noticed the gap and quickly ordered Baxter to "at once ... change front forward on his left battalion, and to close this interval." Baxter immediately obeyed this command and sent the regiments of the 83rd New York Infantry Regiment and the 88th Pennsylvania Infantry Regiment into the gap, thus filling the void, where they rested between the 12th Massachusetts Infantry Regiment and the 97th New York Infantry Regiment. The 90th Pennsylvania Infantry Regiment remained along the Mummasburg Road to protect their right flank, but moved a short distance northward to a more advanced position. General Baxter instructed his men forward to take shelter behind the breastworks running on their left. There, Baxter's men were ordered to lie down and had the colors dipped below as well. Baxter wisely used the lay of the land to shield his troops' position from the rapidly approaching enemy.[19]

On the Confederate front, General Alfred Iverson was leading this attack; he, like O'Neal, decided to stay behind from his command. Captain V. E. Turner of the 23rd North Carolina Infantry Regiment spitefully remembered: "Our brigade commander, after ordering us forward, did not follow us in

John C. Robinson. *(Photo courtesy of library of Congress)*

that advance, and our alignment soon became false." Like the attack by O'Neal's troops, Iverson's also broke off a contingent with his men. Initially, they left their position near the John Forney house and attempted to exploit a gap between the two Federal divisions—the very gap that Baxter had just finished sewing up. However, with their brigade commander watching from the safety at the top of the ridge, this charge too became a disaster.

First Lieutenant George W. Grant of the 88th Pennsylvania Infantry Regiment remembered how he and his regiment quietly awaited the enemy to come within short range. An order soon came down the line as the sea of grey approached their position, telling the Federals to "await the command to fire and to aim low." The order was soon afterwards followed through as the North Carolinians reached effective firing range. Walter Clark, a North Carolina regimental historian, described Iverson's men marching across the field:

> The brigade, about 1,450 strong, advanced under artillery fire through the open grass field in gallant style.... Unwarned, unled as a brigade, went forward Iverson's deserted band to its doom. Deep and long must the desolate homes and orphan children of North Carolina rue the rashness of that hour.[20]

Once Iverson's men got within 50–100 yards, Baxter ordered his men up. Lieutenant Grant remembered that "a death-dealing flame belched forth, staggering them momentarily ... leaving the ground strewn with the dead and wounded." The initial fire from the Federal volley nearly collapsed all of Iverson's left. The regimental historian of the 88th, John Vautier, remembered: "Hundreds of Confederates fell under that first volley, plainly marking their line with a ghastly row of dead and wounded men whose blood trailed the course of their line with a crimson stain clearly discernible for several days after the battle until the rain washed the gory record away." Captain V. E. Turner recalled: "When we were in point blank range the dense line of the enemy rose from its protected lair and poured into us a withering fire..."[21]

Despite being heavily battered by enemy fire, Iverson's Brigade displayed great zeal. While men began to fall, they performed a short fighting withdrawal until they reached a low spot in the ground about 150 yards from the stone wall. Here, the Federal troops "poured down upon [them] a pitiless rifle fire," remembered one Confederate soldier: "Unable to advance, unwilling to retreat, the brigade lay down in this hollow or depression in the field and fought as best it could."[22]

Not long after, the other Confederate troops were compelled to fall back as quickly as possible to the rear, leaving their dead and wounded strewn across the blood-soaked ground. The flight carried most of the retreating troops to a shallow bed of a dry creek, where they continued to take heavy fire from Baxter's force. Unfortunately for Iverson's Confederates, the shallow depth of the trench gave them very little room to hug the ground. Bullets hissed and whizzed over their heads. In some places, they could not even rise to fire their muskets without being struck.

The North Carolinians were caught in the open, no longer possessing the ability to retreat nor to advance on their foe, and they were being decimated by missiles of lead and iron. General Cutler's Brigade now joined in on the slaughter and opened upon the hapless North Carolinians. An infantryman of the 88th Pennsylvania Infantry Regiment recalled witnessing the sad ending of his friend:

> A color-bearer making himself very conspicuous by defiantly flaunting his flag in plain view, Evans remarked, as he brought his piece to his shoulder, "John, I will give those colors a whack." At this moment, Witmoyer heard the dull thud of a bullet, and turning quickly, asked Evans if he was hit. The sergeant did not reply, but slowly bringing his musket down, fell over dead, the ball having pierced his heart.[23]

Grant remembered: "A steady death-dealing fire was kept up, our men loading in comparative safety, and then resting rifle on boulders before them ... would fire coolly and with unerring aim."[24]

Iverson's men eventually succumbed to the relentless fire being dealt upon them. They began to wave handkerchiefs and whatever else they could find implying their surrender. Lieutenant Oliver Williams of the 20th North Carolina Infantry regiment remembered: "I was wounded early in the fight. I believe every man who stood up was either killed or wounded."[25]

General Baxter felt as though this may have been a trap to get the Federals out from their defenses so they could be attacked. Baxter jumped up and said, "Up boys, and give them steel." Douglas Southall Freeman noted that, during the charge, "some of Iverson's men, realizing they were about to be surrounded and slaughtered waved their handkerchiefs in surrender." Iverson witnessed this act and "thought the dead men in the line were alive and were yielding." Baxter's Brigade hurried forward and captured most of Iverson's remaining troops.[26]

Confederate Captain Thomas Toon later lamented:

> General Iverson reports 500, and some 322 surrendered, men his brigade killed, lying in as good order as if on dress parade. Why these men were kept in that position when they could only die without being able to inflict injury on the enemy, I have been at a loss to understand.

Afterward, General Rodes said in is Official Report that "Iverson's men fought and died like heroes."[27]

Most of the blame could be placed squarely on the shoulders of General Iverson himself. J. D. Hufham Jr., of Ramseur's Brigade, stated: "General Ivison [*sic.*], who was drunk, I think, and a coward besides, was off hiding somewhere." Not only due to the retreat, Iverson took scrutiny as to why he had stayed back from his command and simply watched them get slaughtered. He, almost immediately, became heavily ridiculed for his actions, including accusations that he was drunk at the time.

General Rodes would also say of Iverson's attack: "His dead lay in a distinctly marked line of battle." Another witness to the battle, Second Lieutenant Walter Montgomery, of the 12th North Carolina Infantry Regiment, attested that "Iverson's men were uselessly sacrificed. The enemy's position was not known to the troops. The alignment of the brigade was a false one, and the men were left to die without help or guidance. All of the field officers were killed or disabled." General Ewell noted in his Official Report: "The left of Iverson's Brigade was thus exposed, but these gallant troops obstinately stood their ground till the greater part of the three regiments had fallen where they stood in line of battle."[28]

A member of the brigade's burial detail that evening, and also a member of the 23rd North Carolina was found "stone dead" with his musket still in his grasp and five balls through his head, which "attests the close and deadly fire under which they lay." Private Henry Robinson Berkeley, of the Amherst Artillery, wrote of a gruesome sight that he witnessed in his diary of Iverson's dead:

Richard Ewell.
(*Photo courtesy of Library of Congress*)

> I saw a sight which was perfectly sickening and heartrending in the extreme. It would have satiated the most blood-thirsty and cruel man on God's earth. There were, in a few feet of us, by actual count, seventy-nine North Carolinians lying dead in a straight line. I stood on the right and looked down their line. It was perfectly dressed. Three had fallen to the front, the rest had fallen backward; yet the feet of all these dead men were in a perfectly straight line. Great God! When will this horrid war stop?[29]

Colonel Daniel Christie of the 23rd North Carolina Infantry Regiment, who was mortally wounded in Iverson's ill-fated charge, would be taken to a farm near the Mummasburg Road. Here, knowing that the end would soon come, he drew some of the boys near and said that "he might never live to again lead them [into] battle but he would see that 'The imbecile Iverson never should.'" General Iverson would be transferred out of the Army of the Northern Virginia and his reputation would be forever tarnished. General O'Neal, however, would be allowed to stay within the army, even though he lost much of the respect of some of the most senior officers.[30]

After the decimation of Iverson's Brigade, General Baxter's Brigade remained in their advanced position for some time until compelled to fall back again behind the stone wall from whence they came. One regiment

Iverson's Position. (*Photo courtesy of Katie Campbell*)

had a few trophies to boast about as they crossed back to behind the stone wall. The 88th Pennsylvania Infantry Regiment captured the colors of the 23rd North Carolina Infantry Regiment and those of the 26th Alabama regiment. Nevertheless, the fighting was far from over. Although positioned behind the stone wall, there still remained a stiff fire from Confederate sharpshooters. One Pennsylvania soldier remembered that "a head or body shown above the wall became a target, and many fell dead or wounded."[31]

During this time, General Baxter realized that the colors of the 20th North Carolina Infantry Regiment, which the 97th New York had just captured, were being brazenly displayed in front of the Confederates. Fearing that the captured flags may become a prime target for another assault to recapture them, General Baxter ordered Colonel Charles Wheelock, the commanding officer of the 97th New York, to take the captured flags to the rear. Colonel Wheelock replied: "My regiment captured these colors and will keep them." Threatened now with arrest, Wheelock immediately called to a captain from a nearby company and placed the flag staff in the captain's hands and then drove his sword through the flag, tearing it from the staff. Wheelock then waved the torn banner in front of the enemy, making himself an obvious target. A sharp crack from a sharpshooter's rifle soon commenced, and although Colonel Wheelock was unscathed, when hot lead fell around him, the captain he had summoned moments before "received a ball in the forehead and fell dead." After this incident, Wheelock left the field.[32]

With O'Neal renewing his attack, General Gabriel Paul's Brigade had been summoned from near the Seminary. It was here that Major Abner Small of the 16th Maine Infantry Regiment recalled an incident he had with a captain. He attested: "Captain Whitehouse came to talk with me." Small remembered:

> "Adjutant," he said, "I wish I felt as brave and cool as the colonel appears."
>
> "Why, Captain," I said, "he's as scared as any of us. Cheer up! Twill soon be over." He tried to cheer up, and made sad work of it; his face wore a look of foreboding, and his smile was a stiff mockery. While we were talking we heard the command to fall in and he looked at me full in the face and said: "Good-bye, Adjutant. This is my last fight."[33]

Soon after this incident took place, General Paul's Brigade received orders to assume the same shallow "V" formation where General Baxter's troops had been placed, as Baxter's Brigade had now moved to close the gap between them and General Cutler's Brigade.

On the march, General Paul's Brigade crossed over an open meadow and the unfinished railroad cut on their way to the stone wall on Oak Ridge held by Baxter's Brigade where they came under enemy fire. Captain Whitehouse was among those first killed, thus fulfilling his premonition. General Paul's Brigade soon arrived at the stone wall around 3.15 p.m. and moved into position with the 94th New York, 16th Maine, and the 107th Pennsylvania placed to connect with Baxter's right flank to extend his line. The 104th New York and the 13th Massachusetts were placed on the other side of the "V," along the Mummasburg Road, towards the Eleventh Corps line.

It was not long after they had taken their position that General Paul's men met with destruction as well. Captain William Waldron, of the 16th Maine, who was seen shouting to his men to keep cool and aim low, was hit in the neck. Regimental historian and member of the 16th Maine, Abner Small, recalled: "I saw him put up his hand as blood gushed from his neck. He clung to a tree, and stood there stubbornly, keeping his place and refusing to be taken to the surgeons."[34]

Major H. J. Shaeffer, of the 107th Pennsylvania, wrote: "[We] went into action with the determination to conquer or die." The 13th Massachusetts, on the far right flank of Paul's Brigade, were also the targets of some Confederate skirmishers strewn throughout the Moses McClean house and barn. "Here," Lt. William Kimball of Company "A" remembered, "from one of their sharpshooters ... Morris received his mortal wounding." Roland Morris was the color bearer of the 13th Massachusetts Infantry. He was young, handsome, and well liked among his comrades in arms. Kimball went on to describe the young sergeants last moments: "I saw him when he was shot; he leaped into the air and fell to the ground, struggling and crying in agony. The rebel bullet passed through his breast apparently. I detailed two comrades to take him to the rear, and I never saw him again." Morris's wound was fatal.[35]

On Oak Hill, General Junius Daniels' Brigade now began to march forward to assault the Federals' impervious positon. One regiment, the 32nd North Carolina, carried a new flag prototype into battle to be approved by General Lee. The flag would be none other than the famed Second National banner and it gave the men of the 32nd a huge morale boost. One soldier in that regiment later commented after the battle:

> Yes, the bright eyes of our brave boys, which then sparkled with joy and hope, were soon glazed with the stony stare of death; and their joyous shouts and cheers, so eagerly and so proudly greeting the new flag of the young Confederacy, were so soon changed to dying groans and expiring gasps.[36]

General Ramseur would later state that the regiment's "conduct ... carried into the fight that flag with the long white tail to it ... marched as steadily as if on dress parade..."[37]

General Daniel's Brigade had initially marched in support of Iverson's Brigade as planned; however, a slight change in the direction of Iverson's attack put Daniel's troops too far to his right to assist him directly, and Daniel's men had already become engaged with the enemy before being able to make an adjustment in their alignment. The Federals they were sparring with were members of Cutler's already battered brigade and Colonel Roy Stone's Brigade, which had been posted on the other side of the unfinished railroad cut. General Daniel's troops attacked Cutler's Brigade with the regiments of the 2nd North Carolina Battalion and the 43rd, 45th, and 54th North Carolina Infantry Regiments, while Colonel Stone's Brigade was attacked by the 32nd North Carolina Infantry Regiment.

After his regiments assumed their line of battle, General Daniel directed his men towards the unfinished railroad cut in an attempt to break the Federal line, which resulted in driving the enemy from the cut in confusion and compelling their artillery to retire from the McPherson barn. He also gave orders to the 32nd North Carolina Infantry Regiment to press forward and attempt to dislodge the troops positioned near the

The site of Iverson's attack looking from the Federal position. (*Photo courtesy of Katie Campbell*)

McPherson barn. General Daniel also ordered the 45th North Carolina Infantry Regiment and 2nd North Carolina Battalion to shift to the East attack in unison against Stone's defenders.

The Confederate tide marched across the cut and took heavy artillery fire from Lieutenant James Stewart's Battery "B," 4th U.S. "It was more than they could stand," Stewart proudly reported. Moments later, the Confederate tide again advanced. This time advancing farther, yet again Stewart's Battery opened with double canister at 300 yards. He continued in his report: "They broke to the rear ... meeting with such a storm of lead and iron, they broke and ran over the rising ground entirely out of sight."[38]

Again, Daniels rallied his men and advanced with them. Once in position, Daniel had these men keep up a heavy fire, which took terrific effect on the waning Federals and provided him with an opportunity to scout out the area. He saw that the unfinished railroad "could only be carried by moving a force across the cut to support the line advancing on the left ... and that it could only be crossed by moving a regiment by the flank in rear and on the right of [his] position." The problem with making such an attack is that it would essentially be placing those troops right in the way of General Heth's troops, who, at the time, were still lying in wait for orders to also attack.[39]

Daniel realized that he was now in a predicament. Earlier, he sent a request to Hill's troops to advance with him in unison to break the Federal line, but the approval was not given and now Daniel's flank had become partially exposed to flanking fire. General Daniel ordered Colonel Brabble's 32nd North Carolina Infantry Regiment to "advance across the cut, keeping his left on the cut and his line perpendicular to it." Two other regiments of Daniel's Brigade would attack the defenders along the Chambersburg Pike. The 45th North Carolina Infantry Regiment and the 2nd North Carolina Infantry Battalion would also attempt to break through the Federal troops along the Chambersburg Pike.[40]

On the Federal side, before the initial advance of Daniel's Brigade, Colonel Roy Stone's Bucktail Brigade had lined up in a "V" formation, just as General Baxter's Brigade had done on Oak Ridge. The accurate Confederate artillery fire from twenty of Pegram's guns and fourteen of Macintosh's began to scatter shot and shell across Stone's battle line, who aptly reported: "This made my position hazardous and difficult in the extreme." To avoid the artillery fire, Stone quickly ordered the 149th Pennsylvania into the road and to lie down there. He then ordered his other two other regiments, the 143rd and 150th Pennsylvania, to the left of the stone buildings of the McPherson farm to shelter them from the sight of the artillerists as best as they could. Captain J. H. Bassler of the 149th Pennsylvania recalled: "We were now comparatively safe from the battery

Monument to the 149th Pennsylvania "Bucktails." (*Photo courtesy of Katie Campbell*)

on Oak Hill, but, unfortunately, the enemy to the west got a glimpse of our left before we lay down, and, shrewdly guessing our position, at once commenced to drop shells into our ranks."[41]

Stone realized that he and his men were in danger of annihilation from the incessant artillery barrage, and directed the 149th Pennsylvania's colors to move from their place in line to a pile of rails that had been gathered to the left of their position. By doing this, the artillery fire would almost assuredly be directed toward the colors and would alleviate pressure on the regiment's main line. Thus, Color Sergeant Brehm, "having been quietly instructed by an orderly of Col. Dwight, marched in a northwesterly direction and planted the colors ... forming a right-angle."

By actual distance, the colors were only moved forward about 50 yards, and were now placed to the front and left of the line about 150 yards away from the unfinished railroad cut. Captain Bassler remembered: "In this position our flags were plainly visible over the standing wheat, to the battery west of us ... the men lying behind them were hid from their view; and, evidently thinking that the regiment had changed front, they now diverted their fire in that direction. Stone's ruse had succeeded."[42]

By now, General Heth's other two brigades were beginning to advance against Stone's Brigade from the west. These troops were stout men, hailing the states of North Carolina and Virginia, commanded by Colonel John M. Brockenbrough (the 5th, 40th, and 47th Virginia Infantry Regiments and the 22nd Virginia Infantry Battalion) and Brigadier General James J. Pettigrew (the 11th, 26th, 47th, and 52nd North Carolina Infantry Regiments). Colonel Charles Wainwright remembered the moment he saw the long lines of Heth's brigades:

> Somewhere around three o'clock ... a long column of Rebels came out of the wood a mile or so in our front and filed off to our left. This was soon joined by another column, which when they faced into line formed a second line for them. They marched along quietly and with confidence, but swiftly ... [I] am confident that when they advanced they outflanked us at least half a mile on our left. So soon as they were within range I opened on them with the four guns ... but a brigade of the Third Division sent to support the battery persisted in getting in front—that being the commander's idea of supporting.[43]

It was now about 4 p.m. and General Doubleday realized that his First Corps would soon be engaged in a heavy contest. General Lee's force was concentrating upon the battlefield much quicker than that of Howard's, making it almost impossible for him to hold Lee back. He immediately sent Adjutant General E. P. Halstead in an attempt to receive reinforcements from General Howard's Eleventh Corps. General Halstead located General Howard near the Evergreen Cemetery Gatehouse and told him of Doubleday's request. General Howard replied: "Tell General Doubleday that I have no reinforcements to send him. I have only one regiment in reserve." While the regiment he was referring to nearby was the 154th New York Infantry Regiment, Howard actually had an entire division commanded by General Adolph von Steinwehr in reserve on Cemetery Hill. Halstead became slightly agitated at Howard and then even more so when he pointed out enemy troops in line of battle getting ready to mount an assault. General Howard said: "Those are nothing but rail fences, sir!" The adjutant replied: "I beg your pardon, General; if you will take my glass? you will see something besides rail fences." Howard was still in disbelief, however, and had one of his staff officers go and look for himself with his field glasses. Halstead recalled: "The officer looked, and in an instant lowered the glasses, saying; 'General, those are long lines of the enemy!'"

General Howard finally relented, and sent reserves by saying, "Go to Buford, give him my compliments, and tell him to go to General Doubleday's support." When asked as to where Buford might be found, General Howard showed his irritation and snapped, "I don't know! I think he is over this way," as he pointed eastward. In a dash, Halstead was off in search of Buford.[44]

As the shelling continued, Colonel Langhorne Wister of the 150th Pennsylvania Infantry Regiment was approached by a local townsperson named John Burns. The sixty-nine-year-old had served in the War of 1812 and had brought along his flintlock musket to offer his services to the defense of his country. Upon his request to fight, Wister realized that his troops would be heavily engaged within a few minutes and could use all the help he could get. Wister told Burns to ask if the Wisconsin boys could use him where he would be less exposed. Burns went into Herbst Woods and located the troops of the 7th Wisconsin Infantry Regiment and joined the fighting. John Burns would later write: "Oh, I pitched in with them Wisconsin fellers, the Rebs couldn't make anything of them fellers."

Before the day was over, John Burns was wounded three times and was left lying on the battlefield after the Federal forces retreated from Seminary Ridge. In an interesting story, one Confederate soldier advanced towards the wounded elderly man and asked, "Old man, what are you doing here?" Burns replied, "I am lying here wounded, as you see." Soon, after several demands to know the old man's business in this location and in his condition, Burns gave the Rebel a compelling story, saying, "My old woman's health is very poor, and I was over across the country to get a girl to help her, and coming back before I knew where I was, I had got right into this fix and here I am." Fortunately, Burns would eventually make his way home to recover. General Abner Doubleday would later state in his Official Report: "My thanks are specially due to a citizen of Gettysburg named John Burns who ... shouldered his musket and offered his services."[45]

General Junius Daniel's infantry, meanwhile, marched steadily across the open plain and into full view of Colonel Stone, who reported: "From my position I was enabled to trace their formation for at least two miles. It appeared to be a nearly continuous one of deployed battalions, with other battalions in mass or reserve."[46]

Near the Lutheran Seminary, Battery "B" of the 4th U.S Artillery was unlimbered where it could fire down the entire length of the unfinished railroad cut. Lieutenant James Stewart, commander of the battery, ordered Lieutenant Davidson to take a gun and place it directly on the Chambersburg Pike. Stewart then ordered three other guns to be placed on the other side of the unfinished railroad cut. Once in position, Stewart recalled: "I had not long to wait, as we could see the bayonets of the infantry coming over the rising ground ... about six hundred yards." Daniel's troops soon came within range of the Federal artillerymen who opened fire. Stewart stated: "They broke to the rear, where they halted, faced about and advanced again, but meeting with such a storm of lead and iron, they broke and ran over the rising ground entirely out of sight."[47]

Meanwhile, the 149th and the 150th Pennsylvania Infantry Regiments were becoming hotly by Heth's Division who now had the blessing of Lee to advance. Lieutenant Colonel Henry Huidekoper of the 150th Pennsylvania ordered Color Sergeant Samuel Peiffer to the front of the regiment. After Peiffer moved forward to meet the deadly Confederate attack, Huidekoper pointed to the colors and shouted out, "Bucktails, rally on your colors!" Within moments, Peiffer would suffer a mortal wound. Huidekoper would also be wounded before the days fighting was over.[48]

Colonel Walton Dwight, commander of the 149th, reported:

> Colonel Stone ordered me to move my regiment forward and take possession of the railroad cut, about 50 paces to my front; all of which was accomplished in good order and while the enemy were moving over the low ground between the two positions; consequently, our change of position was unknown to the enemy.[49]

The move chased off most of the remaining Confederates and was deemed a good position to hold as long as they could.

Meanwhile, onward came Daniel's Confederate tide, while Colonel Dwight gave his men the order "to take deliberate aim at the knees of the front rank of the enemy as he came up" and described the unfolding battle in his Official Report: "My position was undiscovered by the enemy until he reached a rail fence, 22 paces in my front." Lieutenant Colonel Samuel Boyd of the 45th North Carolina Infantry Regiment soon viewed the flags of the 149th and ordered his men to fire, but it had little to no effect on the Federal defenders as the volley passed harmlessly over the heads of the awaiting defenders. Colonel Dwight ordered his regiment to return fire by battalion and its effect on the enemy was extremely good as Rebels dropped from the initial volley by the score. This event caused the Confederate troops to break and run. However, General Daniels was able to rally his troops and another attack was made. Again, the 149th fired into the Confederates with great effect and again drove them back. Colonel Dwight remembered "the enemy's dead and wounded completely covering the ground in [their] front." The Confederate troops now changed strategy and began to focus the attack on the 149th's left flank. As a result, Dwight ordered his men to fall back to the original line of battle.[50]

For the men of the 149th's color guard, the ruse proved to be costly. The group consisting of John Hammel, Fredrick Hoffman, John Friddell, Henry Spayd, Corporal Frank Lehman, and Sergeant Henry Brehm had positioned itself near the two rail piles. Spayd remembered: "...we were crouching behind the pile of rails to shield ourselves from the aim of the rebel sharpshooters and it was only at intervals that one of our number would rise to take a hurried survey of the long semi-circle of Confederates to the north, northwest and west."

The sharp enemy volley's trapped the men. As Hoffman remembered, it was not long before desperation set in and some grumbled "that [they] had better return to the regiment without orders." Color Sergeant Brehm disagreed and "refused point blank, as his idea of a soldier's duty was to stick to his post as long as he was able unless sooner relieved."

Smoke filled the air around the stranded band of heroes. Sergeant Brehm finally ordered Hoffman to return to the rear and tell them their colors were in danger of being captured. Fred Hoffman was not seen again by the troops—in a matter of moments, he was completely caught up in the confusion of the retreat and failed to carry out the order.

Time was running out for the color guard. The ear-piercing sound of the Rebel yell thundered towards the hunkered men and they realized that time had ran out. Spayd began to flee in one direction. He made it several yards until, looking back, he saw "Lehman, bearer of the State flag, on his knees with his colors stretched across the rail pile and a rebel pulling at them on the other side." Lehman held on for dear life until Spayd came and shot down the would-be Confederate capturer and struck another with the butt of his musket. The blow caused the Confederate to relinquish the flag. Spayd's spirit was full as he picked up the flag and ran a short distance until he was felled with a bullet to his leg. He desperately tried to shove it under him to hide before the oncoming Confederate tide, but it was to no avail.

While this was unfolding, the story of the National colors was also being written in the history books. As they were jumping to their feet, one of the Rebel soldiers was already on top of the rails. Seizing the colors, the Rebel exclaimed, "This is mine!" Brehm replied in contrast, "no by God it isn't!" Brehm grabbed the Confederate—whose name appears to be Sergeant Price (who apparently is the same man who wounded Spayd and captured the State colors)—by the throat and threw him to the ground, with Brehm falling on top of him. The altercation was soon over, and Brehm was on his feet and heading towards the rear. Before long, however, the three fleeing members of the color guard ran right into a hornet's nest of flying lead. Hammel and Friddle both fell with wounds. Hammel's wound, through the stomach, was mortal. Brehm somehow made it through the Confederate line until a shell exploded, mortally wounding him. Bassler, who was wounded and inside the McPherson barn, later wrote: "The last time but one that I saw Brehm, was immediately after he was compelled to surrender his flag. He followed the captor of his colors to the Confederate rear and passed near where I lay.... It would be interesting to know how many shots were fired at the Color Sergeant while making his way across that meadow." Bassler went on to remember that, even though mortally wounded, "his eyes were ablaze with fire." J. T. Lumpkin of the 55th Virginia, Company "C," made the capture of the flag.[51]

During the withdraw of Stone's Brigade, British observer Colonel Fremantle observed General A. P. Hill discussing the bravery of the 143rd Pennsylvania's color bearer, Sergeant Benjamin Crippen, who stopped and shook his fist at the onrushing Confederate tide and was shot in the act of his bravery. Picking up the colors was Owen Phillips, who already obtained possession of one flag. As he went into the town, Colonel Edmund Dana stopped the panicked young corporal. "What are you bringing that off the field for with both flags?" he inquired of his musket. "I am drilled to the use of my gun, but not the flag drill." Dana agreed and said, "Well, well! Drop your gun and hand me the state flag and don't let any man take those colors from you while you are alive and remember brave Crippen."[52]

The battle front was becoming a drastic scene for the Federal Army. Although the First Corps had come up in a very timely fashion and held the ground to the west of town, it had paid a heavy price, the Confederate troops in General Ewell's Second Corps and General Hill's Third Corps were now beginning to make a coordinated direct assault to attempt to break the Federal lines. The valleys and fields were full of thick smoke and flame from the discharging muskets and Stones men had fallen back towards the Seminary.

Meanwhile, General Thomas Rowley had been given command of General Doubleday's old division, so it was not surprising that he was supposed to handle his job perfectly and perhaps Doubleday was expecting too much out of him. Nevertheless, during the fighting that day, Rowley was seen pacing the line almost frantically in an attempt to get his men to adhere to his orders. Colonel Wainwright observed: "As I pushed through the crowd as rapidly as possible, I came across General Rowley. He was very talkative, claiming that he was in command of the Corps. I tried to reason with him, showing that Wadsworth and several others ranked him: but soon finding that he was drunk, I rode on..."[53]

Pettigrew's Brigade remained awaiting their command to advance, while Colonel Chapman Biddle's Brigade awaited them directly in their path, along with Meredith's Iron Brigade. Their point of aim was a gap that existed between the Iron Brigade and Biddle's Brigade of some 300 yards. Therefore, the 47th and 52nd North Carolina pressed toward Biddle's men, while the 11th and 26th North Carolina went up against the Iron Brigade.

Earlier in the day, just east of the Confederate position, Colonel Chapman Biddle's Brigade lost a regiment, the 151st Pennsylvania Infantry

Regiment, due to it being detached to stand in reserve. This put Biddle in a precarious position because, unknown to him, the Confederate force opposing him outflanked him by nearly half a mile and thus threatened both his flanks before the attack even started.

When the order was finally given for Pettigrew to advance, Captain John Thorp of the 47th North Carolina Infantry Regiment remembered the spirit of the brigade on July 1: "The morale of the men was splendid, and while advancing to its first grand charge, it was with the feelings of conquerors." Colonel Henry K. Burgwyn, known as the "Boy Colonel," commanded the 26th North Carolina Infantry Regiment, still awaited his command.[54]

Soon, the enemy's shells began falling in among the ranks and often striking someone near. Thorp recalled: "We were met by a furious storm of shells and canister.... One shell struck the right company, killing three men, and exploding in the line of file closers, by the concussion, felled to the earth every one of them." Before receiving the command to move into the fray, the 26th North Carolina Infantry Regiment took a more modest approach, as one soldier remembered: "The enemy's sharpshooters occasionally reminded us that we had better cling close to the bosom of old mother earth."[55]

Regimental historian of the 26th, George Underwood, also remembered that "General Pettigrew ... was mounted on his beautiful dappled gray. Never before had he appeared to greater advantage." Pettigrew rode up to the 26th North Carolina troops and gave the order, "echelon by battalion, the Twenty-sixth Regiment by the left flank" and the 26th's Colonel Burgwyn shouted, "Forward March!"[56]

Meanwhile, on the right, Major Alexander Biddle of the 121st Pennsylvania Infantry Regiment remembered the advance of the approaching North Carolinians, noting "a large body of them, amounting to a division or more, advanced in two lines toward [them]." He added: "I saw the line of the enemy slowly approaching up the hill, extending far beyond our left flank, for which we had no defense." Nevertheless, his steady and reliable troops maintained good order and as he would later report: "As the enemy's faces appeared over the crest of the hill, we fired effectually into them."[57]

Major Alexander Biddle soon became aware of the changing battle front and finally determined that he was going to be hard-pressed to hold his current position. His flank was about to become overrun by the 52nd North Carolina sweeping across the field, so he quickly ordered his men to change their front to the left to meet them. However, before this order was carried out, his men began to mass together in a clump to escape the withering fire of the enemy. Major Biddle of the 121st Pennsylvania

Infantry rode over in an attempt to take control of the situation and his troops. While doing so, he noticed the color bearers had dropped the regimental flag on the ground. He hurriedly rode over and hoisted it off the ground to further rally his men. While another "Federal officer came in view and rode rapidly forward bearing a large Federal flag." Throp remembered witnessing the officer, Robert P. Cummins of the 142nd Pennsylvania Infantry, as "the scattered Federals swarmed around him as bees cover their queen."

The position that Biddle's Brigade held was beginning to deteriorate as his men were now essentially sitting ducks with the flanking fire being delivered by the 52nd North Carolina Infantry Regimen. Major Biddle later reported that some of the enemy troops were "able to pour in a fire so much heavier than [they] could return that it was soon evident the position was no longer [theirs]." The 121st Pennsylvania was soon ordered to fall back, with one soldier remembering that "[their] men ... at this point used their muskets until, by fast firing, they became so hot they were compelled to drop them. They would take the one nearest them on the ground, rendered useless because the owner of it was dead."[58]

The 121st Pennsylvania had eventually fallen back, thus sealing the fate of the rest of the brigade. The remaining Confederate troops shifted their attack to the line of the 80th New York, which soon fell back as well, and then on to the 142nd Pennsylvania, who, after now being hit from the front and both flanks, withdrew as well.

Both regiments put up resistance as they fell back toward the Lutheran Seminary, but their stubbornness cost them dearly in the casualty department. Included among this statistic was Colonel Cummins, who was struck by a Minié ball soon after taking control of the flag. A small band of his men tried to carry him to safety, but, after a short distance, all but one of the men had been wounded or killed. One of the men that was wounded turned towards the colonel, took his sword to keep it from being captured, and left him on the field. After being captured, Colonel Cummins was taken to the Confederate field hospital that was being established in the nearby Lutheran Theological Seminary. Late in the evening, Cummins condition worsened and he later expired. His last words were a battle-minded delusion when he shouted loud enough to fill the halls: "For God's sake men, rally, we can whip them yet!"[59]

Colonel Biddle's position in Herbst Woods was officially in Confederate hands. Sergeant James R. Balsley, color bearer of the 142nd Pennsylvania, had been wounded three times and remained on the field having relinquished his beloved flag. A Confederate lieutenant soon approached and asked: "Well, Sergeant, what did you fellows come out to fight against us for, anyhow?"

Balsley replied, "We thought it was right to fight for the old flag." The Confederate officer turned and walked several steps away when he said, "Well, Sergeant, never desert the old flag." Soon after, the Confederate officer ordered his men to fetch the color bearer some water after personally giving him a blanket. Sergeant Balsley thought, as the Confederate officer left him on the field, "about the flag and the struggle that was going on in [their] land."[60]

After the collapse of Biddle's Brigade, the Iron Brigade remained posted in Herbst Woods. They had already suffered heavily earlier in the day from General Archer's attacking Tennesseans and Alabamians, and they were ready for more action as another foe approached.

While the rest of Biddle's Brigade were slugging it out, before their retreat, the 151st Pennsylvania was ordered forward to fill up a gap between Biddle's and Meredith's Brigades in an attempt to save the exposed flank of the Iron Brigade. As Lieutenant Colonel George F. McFarland put it: "There was a gap or interval left immediately in our front between the balance of our own brigade and General Meredith's Brigade.... Into this interval the One hundred and fifty-first Pennsylvania Volunteers was ordered ... it advanced and closed."[61]

The 151st Pennsylvania Infantry Regiment was composed of a rough and rowdy bunch of characters but had little combat experience. The regiment had only been in a small skirmish at the Battle of Chancellorsville and, being one of only two nine-month regiments in the Army of the Potomac, was due to go home at the end of the month. Before the advance, Colonel McFarland cautioned his men "against excitement and firing at random.... [He] did not order them to fire a regular volley, but each man to fire as he saw an enemy on which to take a steady aim." McFarland's men heeded his advice and approached onto the scene as the 26th and 11th North Carolina Infantry Regiments were beginning to take effect on the Meredith's Brigade.

During the initial part of their engagement with Meredith's Brigade, the two North Carolinian regiments advanced to within a few yards of the Federal's line as the 151st Pennsylvania marched right into a hornets' nest. The Iron Brigade gradually pulled away, leaving the regiment on their own to face the oncoming Confederate tide. Men on both sides fell in scores; Colonel McFarland remembered that "the fire of the enemy, at least two to one, was very severe and destructive, and [his] gallant officers and men fell thick and fast." While a member of the 26th North Carolina wrote: "It seemed that the bullets were as thick as hail stones in a storm."[62]

During the close-range fighting, Colonel Burgwyn took hold of the 26th North Carolina's battle flag, which had already been dropped several times by enemy bullets, seeking to encourage his men to make a stand. Private

Frank Honeycutt begged Burgwyn to allow him to bear the flag instead. As the Colonel turned to hand Honeycutt the flag, one of the 26th's men remembered what happened next: "Turning slightly to the left to see how they were behaving, a ball entered his left side and passed through both his lungs. He fell with the colors wrapped about him, and with his last breath sent a message to his commander: 'Tell the general my men never failed me at a single point.'" Around the same time that Burgwyn suffered his mortal wound, Honeycutt also was killed by a lead missile to the head. Colonel John R. Lane ran upon the scene to find his colonel barely clinging on to life. "My dear Colonel," Lane said, "are you severely hurt?" The colonel could not utter a word, instead, he grasped Lanes hand tightly and drew his attention to the large wound on his side. Lane later wrote: "The colors, now stained by the noblest blood heroes can shed, lay between the dying colonel and the dead gallant private."[63]

The objective that was behind the plea was to allow them to fall back to the ridge behind them and throw up a rail barricade. According to Dudley, their answer would arrive moments later: "We were occupying the line selected by our corps commanders, and that we must hold it at all hazards."[64]

Things were not better towards the center of the brigade. The 24th Michigan had lost nearly all its color bearers at this time and the flag came twice into possession of Colonel Morrow. Each time he relinquished it to another man of the regiment until that man was taken down by an enemy bullet.[65]

Much of this fire was being delivered by the 11th North Carolina Infantry Regiment and elements of the 26th North Carolina Infantry Regiment. However, two other North Carolina regiments also began to bear down on the hapless 19th Indiana and 151st Pennsylvania. During this fighting, the Iron Brigade lost their commander, General Meredith, when he was wounded in the head. Lieutenant Louis Young of the 26th North Carolina later wrote of the horrors of the fighting in that the deadly wooded area:

> It was a wholly contested field, and the stubborn resistance of the "Iron Brigade" was met with more than equal determination ... the battle raged at forty, then twenty yards between the contestants. In the Twenty-sixth North Carolina, thirteen standard bearers were shot down; and around the flag of the enemy which was planted beside a large tree, the dead and wounded were piled up.[66]

Major John Jones of the 26th North Carolina Infantry Regiment wrote: "The fighting was terrible—our men advancing, the enemy stubbornly resisting, until the two lines were pouring volleys into each other at a distance not greater than 20 paces."[67]

Finally, one last Confederate rush was made up the ridge to take the ground occupied by the Iron Brigade. Lieutenant Young later stated: "I have taken part in many hotly contested fights, but this, I think, was the deadliest of them all." Death and lead swirled around the men of the Iron Brigade as they were now beginning to take a few steps backward due to the mounting pressure. When the Confederates made their final rush, the brigade, along with Colonel Roy Stone's Bucktail Brigade and Biddle's, broke and they retreated back towards the Seminary. Eventually, the victorious Confederate advance stalled as they moved toward the crest of the hill. Here, the attackers would reassemble and two fresh brigades from a different division would attempt to push the Federals from their new defensive position.

The dead and wounded from both the Federals and Confederates lay everywhere throughout the woodlots and fields on the western outskirts of Gettysburg. General Pettigrew alone lost nearly 1,000 men in their efforts to dislodge the enemy. The cries of agony filled the air from high-ranking officers to privates. Among the wounded was the brigade commander who started it all, General Henry Heth.

Heth was struck in the head by a Minié ball, which could have been fatal had it not been for the oversized hat his staff obtained for him in Cashtown during their approach into Gettysburg. One of his aides stuffed the lining of the hat with paper to allow the hat to fit better. That extra padding provided enough cushion to spare the general's life.[68]

7

The Eleventh Corps Collapse

The chain of command in the Federal Army was changing wildly on July 1, and the Eleventh Corps was no exception. With General Hancock on his way, Howard still remained in full command of the field. General Carl Schurz made the move up the command chain to become acting commander of the Eleventh Corps, in charge of its two divisions. General Schimmelfennig, a brigade commander, was assigned temporary command of General Schurz's Third Division.

The Eleventh Corps brought its tarnished reputation to the field with it that morning. Composed primarily of German immigrants, the corps had been routed in prior battles—most recently at the Battle of Chancellorsville, where General Thomas "Stonewall" Jackson had sent an attack on the Federal right flank. The attack succeeded in driving the Eleventh Corps from the battlefield and embarrassment ensued. Now, here on the plains of Gettysburg, they held nearly the same line of battle with the same defensive goal as in May at Chancellorsville, with, hopefully, a different result.

The alignment of the Eleventh Corps was made such as to counter an enemy attack that was reportedly coming from the Harrisburg Road, just north of the town. However, their meager lines were stretched thin due to an advance movement made by General Francis Barlow and his First Division of immigrants.

Having originally been deployed several hundred yards to the rear of Blocher's knoll, which now bears his name, General Barlow recognized the importance of the knoll directly to his front. The argument can be made that Barlow's movement forward was a great benefit of the Eleventh Corps; if Confederate troops of General Ewell's Second Corps troops approaching from the north had captured the high ground there, the Confederates could have used it as an artillery platform and shelled the troops of the Eleventh Corps positioned on the exposed plains south of the knoll. It would later be said that General Barlow must have simply misunderstood the orders given by General Schurz or that Barlow was acting on his own initiative as he advanced forward. General Howard, however, would later state that Barlow positioned his troops as directed and in the accordance with his own orders. Regardless of the reason, General Howard's Eleventh Corps line was ill-prepared to stop much of a Confederate attack. As General Howard would later confess: "Our lines were much extended, and there was quite an interval between the Eleventh and First Corps..."[1]

This interval would be nearly a full quarter of a mile wide, and with such a weakness in the line and accompanied with the fact that the ranks of many regiments were stretched to the point that it was only a single file deep—disaster for the troops in blue seemed a foregone conclusion. Nevertheless, efforts to bolster the Eleventh Corps line were made with the addition of General Schimmelfennig's 45th New York Infantry Regiment and Wheeler's Battery accompanied along with Dilger's.

Just as General Barlow's men moved into position, General Jubal Early's Division could be seen approaching in the distance. Early deployed his men into a line of battle to sweep away whatever may lay in his front after coming into contact with Buford's Cavalry a little earlier. He soon halted his troops on the opposite side of Rock Creek from the enemy defenders and made preparations for the attack.

General John Gordon and his brigade of Georgians were selected to take the knoll. Sergeant Francis L. Hudgins of the 38th Georgia Infantry Regiment remembered: "It was a grand sight to see the Federal infantry on the bank of the stream awaiting motionless our approach. Many a brave fellow on each side of that stream knew full well that in a few short seconds his soul would appear before the God of battle." General Early also recalled his first impressions of the enemy as he gazed upon them: "On the opposite bank of this creek in front of Gordon was a heavy force of the enemy.... Gordon charged rapidly to the front, passing over the fences and Rock Creek and the side of the hill, and engaged the enemy's line on the crest."[2]

General Gordon was a splendid sight in battle. The cool and calm brigade commander rode into battle this day on a black stallion that had been captured during the Battle of Winchester. Confederate Artillerist Robert Stiles recalled: "Gordon was the most glorious and inspiring thing I ever looked upon." Stiles went on to describe the general: "He followed in a trot, close upon the heels of the battle line, his head right in among the slanting barrels and bayonets ... standing in his stirrups, bareheaded, hat in hand, arms extended, and, in a voice like a trumpet exhorting his men. It was superb; absolutely thrilling."[3]

The attacking Confederate force waded across Rock Creek and approached to within 75 yards of their Federal counterparts. Gordon remembered: "The simultaneous appearance of the enemy's battalions on so long a line led me to

John Gordon.
(*Photo courtesy of Library of Congress*)

believe that they had been lying in position for some time behind the woods in our front, fully prepared for us..." Gordon's line pressed in hard on the flank of the Eleventh Corps and the attack was on. However, when they were only a few yards away, the Georgians began to take a withering fire; Hudgins recalled: "We raised the Rebel yell and continued our advance..."[4]

Here an incident occurred involving Major Phil Alexander of the 38th Georgia Infantry Regiment and a Federal soldier whom he ordered to lay down and surrender. The soldier started to comply, and Alexander then ordered another Federal to follow suit. Glancing back at the first man, Alexander saw that he was raising his gun to fire. Alexander quickly turned and struck him with his sword and split the man's head wide open—his gun went off at the same instant, sending a Minié ball through Alexander's hip and the men all lay within a few yards of each other.[5]

Gordon's Georgians attacked the exposed position that the 54th and 68th New York held and broke them with subsequent ease. The New Yorkers began to flee the field, leaving the 153rd Pennsylvania to attempt to support their retreat. Men from both sides fell heavy and quickly, including officers like a captain in the 38th Georgia, William McLeod, who was killed earlier while crossing the creek; even Hudgins himself had taken a wound through his left breast. Hudgins remembered that blood was spurting at every breath from the dreadful wound. Lieutenant

Baxter came over and said to Hudgins: "I think you are about gone up, old fellow." Hudgins, who survived the wound, recalled: "I thought then, and I haven't changed my mind since, that that was the poorest consolation I ever had offered me in my life."[6]

The fighting could be considered by some as hell on earth. Private Reuben Ruch of the 153rd Pennsylvania told his account of the dreadful fighting:

> I fired my gun and as I was taking a cartridge a man behind me was shot. He fell half his length ahead of me, his face toward me. Here was the only time in my life when I tried to look cross-eyed. I was trying to get a cartridge into the muzzle, my gun on my left and watch that fellow dying on my right ... and just at this moment the man on my left was killed ... there was no running but good, solid fighting.[7]

Finally, the 153rd Pennsylvania also received the order to fall back, but the command was still largely ignored by some of the men. Private Ruch happened to be one of those men:

> I did not obey this order with the rest of the regiment, for I was very much interested in the color-bearer ... he was yelling like an Indian. At the time I was returning ramrod ... I thought for a moment I will fix him as soon as I can get a cap on my gun, but while I was placing the cap, I changed my mind.... A Johnnie ... was a little in advance of the wild color-bearer ... and was about reaching for the top rail with his left hand.... When I fired he struck his hand against his side and dropped.[8]

After this incident, Ruch remembered looking back at the pitiful sight that filled his view:

> It presented a regular swath of blue coats, as far as I could see along the line. They were piled up in every shape, some on their backs, some on their faces, and others turned and twisted in every imaginable shape. It presented a picture which will never fade from my memory while I remain on earth—picture which tongue cannot tell nor pen describe.[9]

During all this terrible fighting and bloodshed, it is hard to imagine any humorous stories being tied into the battle. However, Ruch does recall of one that took place during this very time in the battle. As he was falling back though trees and the fields toward town, he ran into Private John Snyder, an older soldier from his company. Snyder was a tall man and hard of hearing and it was said by his fellow soldiers that he could not move faster than a walk, but when Ruch came out of the woods to the field, he witnessed "Snyder in full retreat, with his head drawn down behind his knapsack and his heels flying."[10]

General Von Gilsa's First Brigade had now been driven from the field, which left General Ames' Second Brigade in a bad situation. They too had already been taking fire from sharpshooters and from Dole's Brigade. With Von Gilsa's men now falling back, Ames and his men were now taking fire on multiple fronts just as Biddle's Brigade in Herbst Woods.

It was not long before an order came down from General Ames to the 75th Ohio Infantry Regiment's Colonel Andrew Harris for his men to "fix bayonets, pass to the front between the 107th and 25th Ohio, and if possible check the advance of the enemy." The 17th Connecticut was to follow the 75th Ohio and the objective was to provide some relief to the Federal artillery battery commanded by a nineteen-year-old lieutenant named Bayard Wilkeson that was being hammered by Confederate artillery. Soon after Confederate artillery opened fire on Wilkeson's Battery "G," 4th U.S. Artillery, Bayard was hit by an artillery shell that shattered his leg and killed his horse. Lieutenant Wilkeson withdrew a pocket knife and proceeded to amputate his leg himself before being carried back to the Alms House for medical treatment.

Later that night, Wilkeson asked for a drink of water from one of the aides. After a canteen was given to him, another wounded man who lying near to him begged: "For God's sake give me some!" Wilkeson gave the young soldier the canteen before taking a single swallow himself. The soldier drank the canteen completely empty, not even leaving a drop for Wilkeson. When he peered over towards the young artillery commander, Wilkeson simply smiled, rolled over, and expired.[11]

Not long into the charge, the 17th Connecticut Infantry Regiment's Colonel Douglas Fowler rode forward on his horse ahead of his men. The enemy artillery belched forth their iron almost doubly at the pressed Federal soldiers. Colonel Fowler called out to his troops: "Dodge the big one, boys!" Shortly thereafter, a shell fragment struck Colonel Fowler in the head decapitating him.

The Federal flanks started taking heavy fire and slowly began to break. Looking about, Colonel Harris expected that at any moment he would receive orders to fall back or at least be told that reserves were on their way, but no such order or message ever came. Harris later recalled: "Our situation was perilous in the extreme. We could not advance for our strength was exhausted. Without orders, I hesitated to fall back, but it was soon evident that we could not stay in our exposed condition."[12] Upon seeing that many of his twelve officers lay dead or dying, Harris obliged his instinct and ordered his regiment to fall back without orders to do so. Blocher's Knoll was now in Confederate hands.

General Barlow's men had been driven from the field by Gordon's and Doles' Brigades, but a casualty would take place this day during the retreat from the knoll that now bears his name. In a letter on July 7 to his mother, Barlow stated: "The enemy's skirmishers had hardly attacked us before my men began to run. No fight at all was made." As Barlow attempted to rally his men to form a second line during the retreat, he was wounded by a ball in his side and fell from his horse.

General John Gordon witnessed the young general fall, and reported that he immediately went to Barlow and knelt down to determine how badly he was wounded. He quickly sat him up and saw blood trickling from a bullet-hole in Barlow's back. Gordon grabbed his flask and gave it to the fallen officer and said, "I am very sorry to see you in this condition. I am General Gordon. Please tell me who you are. I wish to aid you all I can." Barlow replied: "Thank you, General. I am Brigadier-General Barlow, of New York. You can do nothing more for me; I am dying." General Barlow paused briefly and came up with something Gordon could do for him and said: "Yes, you can; my wife is at the headquarters of General Meade. If you survive the battle, please let her know that I died doing my duty."[13]

General Gordon replied: "Your message, if I live, shall surely be given to your wife. Can I do nothing more for you?" Another brief pause came over Barlow before he stated: "May God bless you. Only one thing more. Feel in the breast-pocket of my coat-the left breast and take out a packet of letters." General Gordon unbuttoned the now blood-soaked coat and took out the packet. "Now," Barlow said, "please take out one and read it to me. They are from my wife. I wish that her words shall be the last I hear in this world." General Gordon, still kneeling to one side of Barlow, read aloud the letter while the rounds of hissing bullets and screaming shells befell the scenery. When he was finished, Barlow exclaimed, "Thank you. Now please tear them all up. I would not have them read by others." Gordon tore them into bits and threw them across the field.[14]

General Gordon then saddled up to rejoin his command, but before he left, he hastily penned a note to give to General Barlow's wife. The note stated the Barlow was still alive and among the field but seriously wounded. He addressed it to "Mrs. General Barlow, at General Meade's headquarters." Gordon handed it to a member of his staff and told him to place a white handkerchief on his sword and "gallop toward the enemy's line and deliver the note to Mrs. Barlow." The aide obeyed the order and "was not fired upon," and an officer of the Federals rode out to meet him: "...the note was received and read with the assurance that it should be delivered instantly."[15]

This story has been speculated as being untrue, but in the author's opinion, nobody in the present day can accurately ascertain that it did not because, of course, none of us were there at the time of the battle. It is up to you, the reader, to decide whether this account is true or an embellishment

Francis Barlow.
(*Photo courtesy of Library of Congress*)

by Gordon. Whatever the case, Gordon did personally "capture" Barlow and sent him to the rear to receive treatment for his wound.

With one division of the Eleventh Corps being driven off the field, this put General Schimmelfennig's men in a hard spot and Colonel Wladimir Krzyzanwski's Brigade would be sent into the fray. One Ohio soldier remembered them being in support of Dilger's Battery on the Eleventh Corps' left flank:

> The regiment being formed into solid squares by "doubling on the center"…. While the regiment was taking its position, a corporal of my company was struck by one of these missiles and thrown prostrate. Directly another soldier was struck, and the regiment, being unable to return fire, slightly shifted its position. Then the rolls were called, and the men quietly responded to their names amid the boom of cannon and the screech of exploding shells.[16]

During this time, a strong artillery duel ensued involving Captain Hubert Dilger's Battery and Jones' Artillery, firing with great effect. The artillery commander sighted one of the guns himself and dismounted a Rebel gun. Dilger tried again, but at first it looked like his second shot did not cause any damage. After being questioned to the effect of that shot, Dilger then grabbed his spyglass and announced, "I have spiked a gun for them, plugging it at the muzzle."[17]

Near this duel, infantrymen were positioned with shells exploding all around. The nerves of the Federal infantry were understandably becoming frayed since they were terribly outgunned and now facing another assault by fresh Confederate troops. Nevertheless, Krzyzanowski and his men knew what had to be done—advance.

The Federals set forth amid the huge holes being created by the Confederate artillery, and although the gaps were closed, the advance continued. The Federal attack eventually reached to within 200 yards of Doles' infantry line and they were so close that the names of previous battles could be read by the Federals with ease on the Confederate fluttering flags.

General Doles knew that he had a heavy fight on his hands as his men marched into line of battle. John Purifoy, a member of Doles' Brigade, remembered: "The rattle of musketry by the infantry and the roar of Jones's artillery, accompanied with the enthusiastic yells of Confederate troops, were positive evidence that a violent contest was raging." Purifoy also recalled about the advance toward Oak Ridge, that they "marched, in martial array, with banners, flapping defiance to its antagonists."[18]

Captain Theodore Dodge of the 119th New York Infantry Regiment remembered as he began to see the troops in butternut. Their officers were all mounted, waving their swords and cheering on their men. One Federal officer soon said, "Let them have it!" and the troops poured a volley into the advancing Confederates. Doles' men were quick to return fire; one Federal officer recalled: "Bullets hummed about our ears like infuriated bees, and in a few minutes the meadow was strewn with arms and accoutrements, with the wounded and the dead."

Onward the Rebel troops advanced until they were within 100 yards of the Federal position. Captain Dodge recalled:

> Every five or six seconds some poor fellow would throw up his arms with an "Ugh!" and drop; then pick himself up, perhaps, and start for the rear. Another would drop flat on his face, or his back, without a sound; another break down, and fall together in a heap.... One brave boy near me, I remember, shot in the leg, sat there loading and firing with as much regularity and coolness as if untouched, now and then shouting to some comrade in front of him to make room for his shot; while some scared booby, with a scratch scarce deep enough to draw the blood, would run bellowing out of range; or some man, who completely lost his head in the excitement ... would load his musket and deliberately fire in the air.[19]

Here, too, the Confederates drew the upper hand. As one Rebel remembered: "The Federal right gave way, vanishing as mist, for it was a fearful slaughter, the golden wheat-fields, a few minutes before in beauty, now gone, and the ground covered with the dead and wounded in blue." The Rebel line advanced to within 75 yards as the entire Federal line wavered and then broke.

During the retreat, Captain Dodge was wounded in the right foot. As he fell and the Rebel lines went past him, a Confederate soldier stopped and demanded his weapons. Since it was not a lower ranking soldier's right to make such a demand upon an enemy soldier, Dodge told the soldier to "Go to Hell." The straggler then raised his gun to crush the head of Dodge when a Confederate officer intervened. The Confederate officer then requested Dodge's sword, who then complied with the request. The Confederate private then, too, moved on, but not before saying, "D—-d yank, anyhow!"[20]

While Krzyzanowski's men retreated, one of his officers tried to rally his troops. He rose in his stirrups and cried out, "Don't run, men; none but cowards run." Some of the Confederate troops were so much in awe of the bravery that the officer displayed that cries rang out to not shoot him. An attempt was made to capture the brave Federal officer, but before this could be accomplished, the man was hit and tumbled dead from his horse.[21]

Krzyzanowski's demoralized brigade continued to retreat through the town along with the rest of the Eleventh Corps, but not before General Schimmelfennig attempted a last-ditch counterattack to slow the advance of Doles' brigade by using the last regiment he had in reserve, the 157th New York Infantry Regiment. Colonel Philip Brown moved the regiment to within 50 yards of the enemy and squared off against an entire brigade. One of the early Federal casualties was Lieutenant Colonel George Arrowsmith, who was hit in the head. Colonel Brown made his way to young officer and found him "lying upon his back, badly wounded … breathing slowly and heavily, and evidently insensible." Lieutenant Colonel Arrowsmith would die later that day.[22]

The Confederates continued to pound away at the hapless Federal regiment as Colonel Brown remembered: "The men were falling rapidly and the enemy line was taking the form of a semi-circle, evidently with the design of surrounding us." During this time, General Doles was in line of battle with his men when his horse suddenly galloped forward straight at the New Yorkers. The stunned Confederates watched as their commanding officer helplessly rode through their ranks, through the fields, and straight into the line of fire of the enemy. However, just before he reached the enemy position, Doles leaped from the horse and somehow managed to escape capture unscathed.[23]

Colonel Brown soon looked back to see if, by some miracle, supports were on their way, but there were none, and eventually Brown ordered a retreat. The loss of the 157th was fearful as 307 of their men lay killed, wounded, missing, or captured out of 431 that reported for duty that morning.

The Confederate tide had overthrown the Eleventh Corps. The dead and wounded displayed a horrifying sight. Captain Bernhard Domschcke, of the 26th Wisconsin, had been captured in the pursuit. He requested permission to go over to where his regiment had just fought and look over the ground. A Confederate officer permitted this act. Upon reaching his pre-existing location, he found a horrible sight. He explained: "I found many a dear friend dead or wounded ... many cried to me, but I could not help. Some called my name, but blood covered their faces and I could not tell who they were." His heart was full of anguish when he later wrote: "If a man is to be shot, let the bullet smash his head or pierce his heart and dispatch him to eternal rest."[24]

Meanwhile, the attacking Confederate force did not stop there. While General Gordon's Brigade stayed in reserve, it was now time for General Harry Hays's Brigade and Colonel Isaac Avery's Brigade to follow through with an attack on the fleeing Federal tide. In an attempt to check the advance of Early's Division and also cover the retreat of the Eleventh Corps, Colonel Charles Coster's Brigade (composed by the 27th Pennsylvania Infantry Regiment and the 134th New York and the 154th New York Infantry Regiments) was sent from Cemetery Hill to the northern outskirts of town at a small brickyard owned by John Kuhn. Coster could look out and see the advancing Confederate troops and knew that soon his small 920-man brigade would be attacked by the nearly 2,500 troops of Early.

With Coster's Brigade was Captain Lewis Heckman's Battery "K," First Ohio Light Artillery. As Heckman was taking the field, he realized that the enemy was already in range of his own guns. He reported: "I unlimbered, and commenced firing as soon as possible, as the enemy was close to me and advancing."[25]

It did not take long for the Confederates to make quick work of the Federal infantry, which soon became outflanked and their line began to melt away. Avery's troops flanked the right flank of the line defended by the 134th New York, while Hays' men attacked the left flank defended by the 27th Pennsylvania. To make matters worse, the 6th North Carolina also came straight the middle of the line defended by the 154th New York. Most of the men of Coster's Brigade who were not wounded or killed were soon captured. George Mason of the 154th New York recalled: "We have had a hard fight and our regiment was almost taken prisoner ... the few that did get away were the best runners and the most exposed to danger." Of the 920 men brought to the field that day, only 359 were left to answer roll call that night. The Confederate line had once again been victorious against the Eleventh Corps.

As the fields north of Gettysburg had the sound of gunfire replaced with the cries and groans of the wounded, the Federals continued to flee through the streets of Gettysburg. General Schimmelfennig had his horse shot out from under him but was able to find safety in an outbuilding of the Henry Garlach home on Baltimore Street. He remained there during the rest of the battle.[26]

8

The First Corps Collapse

While the Eleventh Corps were fighting north-east of their position, the First Corps had now completely fallen back from McPherson Ridge to the ground just in front of the Lutheran Theological Seminary on the aptly named Seminary Ridge. Covering their left flank was Colonel William Gamble's Federal cavalry, as well as Devin on the opposite flank.

First Corps Artillery Commander Colonel Charles Wainwright had begun to prepare his guns for one last defensive stand. If the line broke again, the Federal troops would have to retreat through the streets of the town to hopefully regroup at a further rally point in the rear. While placing his guns and with General Doubleday nearby, Wainwright received a visitor. It was one of General Howard's aides relaying his orders that "Cemetery Hill should be held at all hazards." Unfortunately for Wainwright, the aide sent did not speak English very well and he had thought the aide said Seminary Hill. Having no idea if a Cemetery Hill even existed, Wainwright began to prepare to hold the ground on which he stood at all costs with his eighteen guns and no reserves.[1]

A fresh division of Confederate infantry under General William Dorsey Pender was now preparing to attack. General Abner Perrin's Brigade (composed of the 1st, 12th, 13th, and 14th South Carolina Infantry Regiments) overlapped the left flank of the First Corps defenders. General Alfred Scales' Brigade (composed of the 13th, 16th, 22nd, 34th, and 38th North Carolina Infantry Regiments) would assault the right flank.

The battered Federals were entrenched behind breastworks, which were hastily thrown up earlier in the morning, and were staying low while awaiting their attackers. Colonel Rufus Dawes of the 6th Wisconsin Infantry Regiment remembered: "Along Seminary Ridge, flat upon their bellies, lay mixed up together in one line of battle, the 'Iron Brigade' and Roy Stone's 'Bucktails.'"[2]

The attack soon came, and Colonel Wainwright recalled: "The Rebs were coming steadily on down the ridge in front only some five hundred yards off ... all the guns were blazing away at them as lively as possible." Wainwright ordered Captain James Cooper and his Battery "B," 1st Pennsylvania Light Artillery, to deliver an enfilading fire on the oncoming enemy lines. "His round shot, together with the canister poured in from all the other guns," wrote Wainwright, "was cutting great gaps in the front line of the enemy. But still they came on."[3]

Finally, the moment was reached when Scales' men were in range of the Federal infantry that awaited them. Colonel William Robinson of the 7th Wisconsin Infantry Regiment remembered that he had some difficulty in restraining his men from firing until they got within range across the open fields in front of their position. Once they were, the order was given and their ranks went down like grass before the scythe from the united fire of the Federal infantry and artillery. Lieutenant Colonel George W. Flowers of the 38th North Carolina Infantry Regiment remembered that initial volley: "The regiment being on the flank, encountered a most terrific fire of grape and musketry in front. Every discharge made sad loss in the line, but the troops pressed on double-quick..."[4] The sight was equally disturbing for the 14th South Carolina Infantry Regiment in Perrin's Brigade. One soldier remembered:

> At the charge bayonets, the enemy were behind a rock fence, and we could hear their officers distinctly encouraging their men to hold their fire, until the command to fire was given. They obeyed their command implicitly, and rose to their feet and took as deliberate aim as if they were on dress parade, 34 of our 39 men fell at the first fire of the enemy.[5]

James F. J. Caldwell, of the 14th South Carolina, recalled that the field "was thick with wounded hurrying to the rear, and the ground was grey with dead and disabled." As casualties began to mount, the Rebels began to waver under the Federal's withering fire and were ultimately compelled to fall back to the wooded line from whence they came. The Federal troops began yelling in a taunting fashion: "Come on, Johnny! Come on!"[6]

Not long after that, the Confederates obliged and renewed their attack. Again, they were met with a shower of leaden missiles. One Federal soldier stated: "The severity of this fire staggered and checked Perrin and almost annihilated the left of this brigade, his troops being wholly swept away from the front of our guns." Colonel Perrin, seizing the initiative, rode his horse through the regiment and led a charge directly into the gap between Gamble's cavalry and Biddle's 121st Pennsylvania Infantry Regiment. Caldwell stated: "Filled with admiration for such courage as defied the whole fire of the enemy, the brigade followed, with a shout that was itself half a victory."[7]

Scales' men were charging so rapidly that some men began to pitch their knapsacks and blankets in an attempt to keep up. The men were "struggling and panting, but cheering and closing up, they went, through the shell, through the balls, heeding neither the dead who sank down by their sides, nor the fire from the front which killed them, until they threw themselves desperately on the line of the Federals..." In this chaos, the Confederate troops had found a soft spot in the Federal line—between Gamble's Cavalry and the Biddle's Brigade—and now exploited it, causing a chain reaction as one Federal regiment at a time fell back in the same fashion as it did in Herbst Woods.[8]

Colonel Dawes was directing the fire of the 6th Wisconsin when Lieutenant Clayton E. Rogers, one of General Wadsworth's aides, came riding up: "The orders, colonel, are to retreat beyond the town.... Hold your men together." The order took Colonel Dawes by surprise. His men had been fighting hard, as had everyone along that part of the Federal line on Seminary Ridge, but what Dawes did not realize was that the line had broken. Dawes ordered his men to about face and fall back in good order.[9]

The same could be said of the men of the 151st Pennsylvania Infantry Regiment. As the order to fall back had reached them, Colonel McFarland positioned his remaining soldiers behind the main Seminary building to shelter them from the fire being delivered by the 14th South Carolina Infantry Regiment. As McFarland crouched down to look under the smoke being emitted by their muskets to see what was going on, he was wounded in both his legs and was carried by Private Lyman D. Wilson of Company "F" to the main Seminary building where his right leg would be amputated.

The same could not be said for many of the other Federal regiments that retreated from their breastworks along Seminary Ridge that day. The 121st Pennsylvania Infantry Regiment fell back without "a semblance of order ... fleeing through the town, on their way to Cemetery Hill as fast as possible."[10]

Colonel Wainwright, who still was not aware of the order to retreat and under the impression that he was to hold the ground at all cost, rode over to the 5th Maine Battery and found them limbering up. Wainwright inquired as to who gave the order to fall back. Artillerist Lieutenant Whittaker told him that "General Wadsworth had said they had better withdraw."[11]

Wainwright, like Dawes, believed they were carrying the day and the order to retreat made no sense. An officer soon rode over to him and informed him that the Confederate line was advancing on their left and the First Corps was now in a full retreat. Wainwright's heart sank as he turned and "ordered all to limber up and move at a walk toward the town." He would not allow them to trot for fear of creating a panic among the infantry and gradually fell back.[12]

At this point, the brigades of Generals Paul, Baxter, and Cutler, north of the unfinished railroad cut, were still holding out even while taking fire from three different Confederate brigades. When the Eleventh Corps line broke, Paul's men came under a dangerous fire from their right flank. General Paul himself became a casualty when a ball passed behind one of his eyes and came out the other, completely blinding him early in the conflict.

Now, a fourth brigade—that of General Stephen Ramseur—poured onto the field and struck near the spot where General Gabriel Paul had refused his line with the 104th New York. The Federal brigade commanders realized the new threat and looked to remedy it by calling up for supports, but there were none. All of the supports had fallen back toward the rear and they were in a very real danger of being completely surrounded and cut off from the main body of the Army of the Potomac. The order finally came to retire.

The 16th Maine Infantry Regiment was getting ready to fall back with the rest of the brigade when one of General Robinson's aides came with an order telling them not to retreat but to advance and hold Oak Ridge as long as possible to support the brigade. Colonel Charles Tilden, the regiment's commander, found this order to be ridiculous and awaited confirmation of the order. Moments later, he received it—his division commander himself rode to Tilden and repeated the order. Colonel Tilden protested: "Our regiment without support couldn't hold the ridge, we numbered fewer than two hundred, all told; as well set a corporal's guard to stop the Rebel army." The general glared sharply at the colonel and told him in a booming voice, "Hold it at any cost!" The bewildered colonel turned about and drew a gaze upon his men and said, "You know what that means." In the same breath, he ordered them to advance to the Mummasburg road.

There, at the corner of the road, they planted their colors. As soon as they arrived in position, Major Abner Small watched as a "line of battle showed up across the way; [they] heard distinctly the commands of the Rebel officer directing his men to fire; and a volley crashed, and [they] saw some of [their] men fall. [Their] line blazed away in reply, and the Rebel flag went down, and the officer pitched headlong in the stubble."[13]

As the men of the 16th Maine peered across the field, they noticed another line of Confederates coming behind the one already attacking them. With no hope, the 16th began a fighting withdrawal and soon lost one of its captains and several other men. Still, slowly and steadily, the regiment fell back, turning to fire on occasions, eventually falling back into the unfinished railroad cut, where the men attempted to drag out their stay just a few moments longer to buy more time for the rest of the men in Robinson's Division. It did not take long for the Confederate troops to pour into the cut a little to the west of the 16th Maine's position and advance toward them.

Now surrounded, the men of the 16th looked with pride at the banner that they served under since their enlistment, and after a quick appeal from the color bearers to the colonel to prevent the regimental colors from being captured, "they tore the flags from their staves, and ripped the silk into shreds; and [their] officers and men that were near took each a shred." Thus, the flag was saved and would not fall into the hands of the enemy. With nothing left to lose, some of the men were somehow able to avoid capture, making it to safety back on Cemetery Hill to what was left of their division. Out of the 298 men and officers who went into battle that day, only thirty-five made it to safety.[14]

The Federals had been beaten and were now fleeing through the town. While in retreat, the 6th Wisconsin Infantry Regiment found the enemy had started to encircle them in a horseshoe-like fashion. Using the Pennsylvania College buildings as a screen, they continued through the streets until they could see other Federal troops retreating ahead of them. By now, the enemy had many of the streets completely blocked. Dawes was able to locate a pen where a large hole had been cut at the base to allow hogs in. Dawes, with colors in hand, instructed his men to follow him into the pen. Fortunately, the enemy troops blocking the way eventually withdrew and Dawes' regiment were able to continue their retreat and eventually made it to Cemetery Hill and safety.

The 45th New York Infantry Regiment became separated from the main body of the Eleventh Corps as they retreated through the town. When the enemy began to advance on them, and with it seeming as though they would all be captured, Captain Francis Irsch gathered his three or four companies and made a last stand in several buildings around the intersection at Chambersburg and Washington Street. Finally, a Rebel officer came to them with a flag of truce and requested their surrender. Captain Irsch originally refused to do so because he "expected every moment to be relieved, as the Army of the Potomac was coming on." The Confederate officer simply shook his head and said, "The whole town was in the possession of the Confederates." He offered Irsch "safe conduct" and let him look for himself. As Irsch peered out, he saw General Ewell on horseback riding over to the officer making an attempt to capture Irsch. He said "in hot haste" that General Lee wanted them to "proceed to attack the Federals on Cemetery Hill..." Ewell paused and spoke a little lower and went on to explain to the would-be captor that "if General Lee knew the condition of his ... troops, after their long march and the fight that had just taken place, he would not think of such an order, and that the attack could not be risked."[15]

Subsequently, the Confederate officer took Irsch on a tour of the surrounding streets and realized his situation was hopeless. Satisfied of the hopeless situation, Irsch agreed to surrender his men. Before doing so, he had his men destroy their weapons and throw them into wells.

Confederate officers were soon focusing on capturing as many Federals as possible, and men were requested to go through Gettysburg to try and secure "such of the enemy as might be lurking there." In the town square, the flag of the 1st South Carolina Infantry Regiment flew on the flag pole. This showed once and for all that the town of Gettysburg had fallen into Confederate hands.

While this was going on, the flag of the 150th Pennsylvania Infantry Regiment fell into the hands of the Confederates after a stiff fight on High Street after its bearer, Joseph Gutelius, refused to surrender its flag. Having been wounded once, he stopped for a rest and was soon surrounded by soldiers from North Carolina. After flat out refusing to surrender the cherished banner, a single volley was fired. Gutelius was dead, and the flag was captured by the 14th North Carolina's Lieutenant F. M. Harney. Eventually, the flag was sent to President Jefferson Davis as a war prize and, later in the war, when he was captured in Georgia, the flag was found with him.[16]

In the 154th New York Infantry Regiment, a father of three children had been mortally wounded while retreating after the fighting at the John Kuhn brickyard just north of the town. His body was found near the Judge S. R. Russell property, clutching a daguerreotype of his three young children. He was originally classified as an unknown soldier and just another casualty of the battle until a photograph of the daguerreotype appeared in newspapers throughout the North and was finally identified by his wife. The unknown soldier of Gettysburg now had a name—Sergeant Amos Humiston—and his body would eventually be interred at the Soldiers' National Cemetery.

At some point in their advance, General O'Neal rode up to General Doles and "requested him to take charge of the division and drive the Federals from the cemetery ridge." General Doles, however, refused to do any such thing without orders. O'Neal remained persistent: "The Federals were demoralized, and we would have no trouble in carrying the ridge." Doles realized the opportunity but still would not advance without the proper clearance. As one officer put it, "It was a fatal mistake." The delay allowed for the Federals to fortify Cemetery Hill and make it into a formidable defensive position with relative ease.[17]

J. E. B. Stuart.
(Photo courtesy of Library of Congress)

General A. P. Hill later stated: "Under the impression that the enemy were entirely routed, my own two divisions exhausted by some six hours 'hard fighting, prudence led me to be content with what had been gained, and not push forward troops exhausted and necessarily disordered, probably to encounter fresh troops of the enemy." General Hill had a point. Due to General J. E. B. Stuart's continued absence, there was no way of knowing what was in his front to press forward, and without knowing that prudent information, any further attack would be extremely risky.[18]

9

Hancock Takes Over

On Cemetery Hill, the retreating Federal troops continued pouring onto its slopes. Some were heading farther to the rear when a familiar face was just then coming into town around 4.30 p.m. It was none other than General Winfield S. Hancock, commander of the Second Corps. As he arrived, General Hancock rode over to Colonel Orland Smith of General von Steinwehr's Division and, after briefly complimenting Colonel Smith and his men, stated: "My corps is on the way, but will not be here in time. This position should be held at all hazards. Now, Colonel, can you hold it?" "I think I can." the colonel replied. That was not the answer Hancock was looking for and again he asked, "Will you hold it?" To this, the answer that he was looking for came, "I will."[1]

As Major Abner Small and his men arrived on Cemetery Hill, he remembered that this was one of the first instances they noticed was Hancock personally directing the placement of troops. Hancock found that the fighting for the day was essentially over, and located General Howard near the Evergreen Cemetery Gatehouse. Hancock saluted Howard and began to explain that he was now in control of the battlefield as a result of General Meade's order. Howard spoke of how he was the senior officer, to which Hancock responded, "I am aware of that, General, but I have written orders in my pocket from General Meade, which I will show you if you wish to see them."[2]

With a stern refusal, Howard said, "No; I do not doubt your word, General Hancock, but you can give no orders here while I'm here." Hancock grew a little restless while attempting to remain as calm as possible: "Very well, General Howard. I will second any order that you have to give, but General Meade has also directed me to select a field on which to fight this battle.... But I think this the strongest position by nature upon which to fight a battle that I ever saw.... I will select this as the battlefield."[3]

General Howard could not agree more with Hancock about the military value of Cemetery Hill. Scanning over toward Culp's Hill and then the

Winfield Hancock.
(Photo courtesy of Library of Congress)

Round Tops, Howard commented: "I think it a very strong position, General Hancock; a very strong position!" Despite this small conflict between the two higher ranking officers in the army, General Carl Schurz remembered that Howard cooperated so professionally with Hancock that it would have been hard to tell which one was the commander and which one was the subordinate. The two worked in tandem together in the placement of the troops as the men began to file into their lines.

Colonel Orland Smith's Brigade was quickly positioned on Cemetery Hill and his troops were followed by more as they arrived: Coster's Brigade, then General Ames' Brigade, and then General Schurz's Brigade. General Hancock sought out Colonel C. H. Morgan and sent him with orders to have General Doubleday, and the remnants of his First Corps, move and occupy Culp's Hill. Hancock clearly realized that if the Confederates occupied that hill, it could be readily used as an artillery platform and used to shell the Federals on Cemetery Hill and likely be able to force them off it.

Colonel Morgan found Doubleday and gave him the order. The general protested that his men were worn out, cut up, and had no ammunition left. When Hancock was informed of the rejection to the order, he personally went to Doubleday and roared, "General, I want you to understand that I am in command here, send every man you have!"[4]

After time had passed and he was satisfied of the troop placements, and knowing that General Henry Slocum's Twelfth Corps would soon be arriving on the field, Hancock reported to General Meade of the current condition of the troops and their positions. With the battle plan of Pipe Creek still on his mind, Hancock reported to General Meade: "I think we can retire; if not, we can fight here, as the ground appears not unfavorable with good troops." Hancock sent his senior aide, Major Mitchell, to Meade, still located in Tanytown, MD.[5]

General Howard had also reported to General Meade about a half hour before Hancock. Instead of simply telling of the commanding position the Federal Army held (on Cemetery Hill), Howard resorted to finger pointing, especially at General Doubleday and his First Corps, blaming them for the collapse of the entire Federal line that afternoon. The blame game did not stop there with Howard. He also spoke to Hancock about Doubleday's retreat, which Hancock mentioned had in his report to General Meade. As a result, Meade replaced Doubleday as commander of the First Corps with General John Newton, who was commanding the Third Division of the Sixth Corps. General Doubleday never did forgive Howard for metaphorically "throwing him under the bus."

The feeling of many of Meade's subordinates that Gettysburg was the place to fight this battle helped General Meade to finally scrap his Pipe Creek battle plan: "Turning to General Seth Williams, his adjutant-general, he said: 'Order up all the troops, we will fight there!'"[6]

Towards evening, after having accomplished much in his short time on the field, Hancock walked among a line of breastworks and sat down on the stone fence that overlooked a field below. General Schurz soon joined him and both sat and watched the somewhat confusing movements of the enemy troops. General Schurz admitted that he was nervous but said, "It was soothing to my pride, but by no means reassuring as to our situation, when General Hancock admitted that he felt nervous, too." The two discussed the next day's assumptions before eventually retiring for the night.

Years later, General Schurz wrote of that night:

> There was nothing of extraordinary solemnity in the 'goodnight' we gave one another when we parted. It was rather a commonplace, businesslike 'good-night' as that of an ordinary occasion. We of the Eleventh Corps, occupying the cemetery, lay down, wrapped in our cloaks, with the troops among the grave-stones. There was profound stillness in the graveyard, broken by no sound but the breathing of men and here and there the tramp of a horse's foot; and sullen rumblings mysterious floating on the air from a distance all around.[7]

On the Confederate side, as the sun was beginning to set, General Robert Rodes pondered the idea of whether to pursue the enemy and continue his push. He gazed at his exhausted troops (having already lost around 2,500 men), reminded himself of General Lee's order to not bring on a general engagement, and decided to halt his attack. He then went to try to find someone who may know what further orders were forthcoming. Rodes found General Early in town, awaiting orders as well.

General Early's troops had suffered far less casualties than that of Rodes' Division and still kept pursuing the fleeing Federal troops and wished to "advance upon the enemy, before he could recover from his evident dismay and confusion." General Early clearly felt that he could capitalize on their gains that they had already made that day, and convinced Rodes to reconsider his position on the matter. The two then rode off to find General Ewell, their corps commander, to obtain permission from General Lee to proceed with attacking Cemetery Hill.[8]

A few moments later, they found Ewell and made their request with urgency. Almost without hesitation, Ewell turned to Captain James Power Smith, who served on General Thomas "Stonewall" Jackson's staff until Jackson's death at Chancellorsville, and said, "Captain, you have lately left General Lee; perhaps you can find him again. Please tell him what Generals Early and Rodes wish to say." Captain Smith rode off in his search.[9]

Not long after Smith's departure, Colonel Walter Taylor, of Lee's staff, rode up with instructions for Ewell and ordered him to carry the hill occupied by the enemy if he found it practicable, but to avoid a general engagement until the arrival of the other divisions of the army, which were ordered to hasten forward. General Lee's orders carried yet another contradiction throwing Ewell into confusion.

While the generals discussed the order, General Ewell had been informed that "Extra Billy" Smith, who had been guarding the rear flank of the division with his brigade, had reported "that the enemy was advancing a large force of infantry, artillery, and cavalry on the York road, menacing [their] left flank and rear." General Early turned toward Ewell and said, "General, I don't much believe in this, but prefer to suspend my movements until I can send and inquire into it." As a precautionary measure, Early then sent General Gordon's Georgians out the York Pike to assist in covering the division's flank. As a result, General Early now found himself with only two of his brigades to make an assault on Cemetery Hill if he decided to make one.[10]

Meanwhile, General James P. Longstreet, Lee's "Old Warhorse," had also arrived at Gettysburg and found his way to Lee's headquarters, across the street from Mary Thompson's house. While there, Longstreet took his field glasses and began to study the enemy's position and the lay of the land surrounding the town. Longstreet noted that Lee "seemed under a subdued excitement which occasionally took possession of him when 'the hunt was up' and threatened his superb equipoise. The sharp battle fought by Hill and Ewell on that day had given him a taste of victory." Lee was still very adamant about not engaging the enemy until all his troops were up, but like Meade, the battle had already begun to take a life of its own and the choice seemed to be his. Colonel Walter Taylor, of Lee's staff, remembered: "General Lee witnessed the flight of the Federals through Gettysburg, and up the hills beyond." The scent of victory was in the air and Lee wanted to exploit their losses the best way he could—by attacking.[11]

General Longstreet soon turned to General Lee with great joy saying, "We could not call the enemy to position better suited to our plans. All that we have to do is to file around his left and secure good ground between him and his capital." Longstreet's plan to disengage the enemy and swing around toward Baltimore and Washington, D.C., would have forced Meade into an aggressive state of mind, and it would have produced

James Longstreet. (*Photo courtesy of Library of Congress*)

great political pressure upon the Federal commander to attack the new Confederate position. Longstreet wrongly believed that Lee was under the mindset that there would be no aggressive battle fought on the enemy soil and that Lee's plan would coincide with Longstreet's defensive strategy.[12]

Much to General Longstreet's surprise and dismay, Lee struck the air with his closed fist exclaiming, "If he is there tomorrow, I will attack him." Longstreet replied, "If he is there, it will be because he is anxious that we should attack him! A good reason in my judgment for not doing so." He then began to press Lee again about his earlier suggestion to move all the Confederates troops around Meade's left and take up a strong defensive position on ground of their own choosing. Choosing his words carefully, Longstreet said that the enemy "was in strong position and would be awaiting [them]," and for emphasis, Longstreet pointed his finger at the Federal position and declared that the ground was more favorable for a defensive approach than an aggressive one by the them.[13]

General Lee was not hearing any of it. In his mind, it was now or never. After seeing that he had not convinced him, Longstreet added: "If we carried the heights in front of us, and drove Meade out, we should be so badly rippled that we could not reap the fruits of victory." Lee still was not convinced and Longstreet finally returned to his camp under the impression that "he made up his mind to attack, but had not yet determined as to when the attack should be made."[14]

About that same time as the sharp disagreement between Longstreet and Lee kicked off, Captain Smith delivered General Ewell's request. Smith explained the situation to Lee that "it would be well for him to occupy at once the higher ground in front of [their] right." General Lee pointed toward his front and said, "I suppose, captain, this is the higher ground to which these gentlemen refer?" After Smith nodded, Lee handed his field glasses to Smith and remarked, "You will see that some of those people are there now." Looking over the area, Smith witnessed a number of mounted Federals and other miscellaneous signs that indicated a military presence on the hill.[15]

Lee then stated: "Our people are not all up yet and I have no troops with which to occupy this higher ground." After he turned and asked General Longstreet when he could have his corps up, Longstreet replied that McLaws' men were still about 6 miles away. Lee then directed Smith to tell Ewell that "he regretted that his people were not up to support him on the right, but he wished him to take the Cemetery hill if it were possible: and that he would ride over and see him very soon."[16]

With that statement, the opportunity was lost to drive off the Federals from hill. Years later, General Hancock stated: "In my opinion, if the Confederates had continued the pursuit of General Howard on the afternoon of the first day of July, they would have driven him over and beyond Cemetery Hill."[17]

Meanwhile, General Early went to Hays, who pointed out the importance of Culp's Hill and to "not only occupy it, but capture the Baltimore Pike." General Early too witnessed what Hays had seen and in agreement said, "I am satisfied that you are right; it should be occupied on the spot but I cannot disobey orders." Early then turned away from Hays and said to himself, but was clearly heard by the men around him, that, "If Jackson were on the field I would act on the spot."[18]

Before the return of Captain Smith, General Ewell began to swing his divisions around to face the more appeasing target of Culp's Hill instead of Cemetery Hill. Ewell, in his Official Report, stated that Cemetery Hill "was not assailable.... and [he] determined, with Johnson's division, to take possession of a wooded hill on [his] left," while deciding to also send a two-man scouting squad to the area for reconnaissance purposes. They were Lieutenant Thomas Turner and Early's nephew, Captain Robert Early. Turner remembered: "It was about 5 p.m. that General Ewell ordered Lieutenant Early and myself to ride up Culp's Hill and ... reconnoiter the enemy's position from its summit." The two men climbed the rugged wooded hill and found that no troops had yet occupied it. However, as mentioned earlier, the Iron Brigade had been directed there by General Hancock. Either the two officers had not seen an entire brigade due to the nature of the hill and the darkness that surrounded them or they had arrived there just before the troops took the hill. Whatever the case, the two men rode back to Ewell with the impression that Culp's Hill was empty of Federal troops and certainly assailable.[19]

Upon their return, Lieutenant Turner and Captain Early found Ewell sitting in a fence corner with Rodes and Ewell and reported their findings. Ewell turned to Rodes and asked what he thought of sending General Johnson up to the top of Culp's Hill. Rodes replied that the men were tired and he did not think it would result in anything one way or the other. Ewell then turned to Early and asked the same question. Early replied: "If you do not go up there tonight, it will cost you 10,000 lives to get up there tomorrow."[20]

By the time that Turner and Early departed, General Johnson had finally reached Gettysburg and reported to Ewell. Ewell inquired as to how far off his division was which was reported that his troops were about a mile away from Gettysburg, and that because they had already marched 25 miles that day, it may be another hour before his troops would get into the desired position. Ewell then turned to Early and asked him if he could use Hays and Avery's Brigades to take Culp's Hill and, when Johnson's Division arrived, they would assume Early's position on the battlefield.

Early scoffed at Ewell's suggestion and said that his command had been doing all the hard marching and fighting and was not in condition to make such a move. The remark was taken personally by Johnson who fired back with strong words of his own. Ewell eventually broke up the argument and ordered Early to make camp and Johnson to bring his men up as fast as possible.

It seemed as though Early's momentum had evaporated. He clearly had enough men to advance up Culp's Hill and take it that night, occupied or not. While it is true that his troops did do much of the hard fighting that day, he still retained enough manpower to drive a single battered Federal brigade off the hill. By the time Johnson's Division arrived, it was almost dark. When Early was originally asked if he could take Culp's Hill, there were more than two hours of daylight left. Instead, Johnson's Division was ordered toward Culp's Hill under the guidance of aides Turner and Early while combating the darkness. As Ewell said in his Official Report: "Johnson [was] placed in position, the night was far advanced." Before leaving, Ewell ordered Johnson to take Culp's Hill if he found it unoccupied.

By this time, things had begun to quiet down around Early's and Rodes' camps. Johnson's Division was still on the march toward Culp's Hill when General Lee arrived at Ewell's headquarters. At one point in the ensuing conversation, the commanding general looked upon Ewell, Rodes, and Early and stated that he "wanted to go forward at dawn the next day, though Longstreet should not be up," to which Lee's subordinates opposed, stating that they should await Longstreet's arrival.[21]

The consensus among the subordinates was that the next day's attack should be made on two different fronts, thereby limiting the chance of Federal reinforcements—effectively moving in and stopping either or both attacks. General Lee agreed, but still wanted to attack as early as possible; he turned to Ewell and asked, "Can't you, with your corps, attack on this flank at daylight tomorrow?" General Early was the first to speak, having passed through Gettysburg almost a week earlier and having the best idea of the lay of the land. He commented:

> The ground over which we would have to advance on our flank was very rugged and steep; ... the enemy was then evidently concentrating and fortifying in our immediate front, and by morning would probably have the greater part of his force concentrated on that flank and the position strongly fortified.[22]

Early stated: "The result of an attack there might be doubtful, but if successful it would inevitably be at very great loss." General Early then pointed out the Round Tops along the outskirts of town, which could barely be seen through the still night air, and added, "Those heights must evidently command the enemy's position and render it untenable ... the attack could be made on that side, and from [the] right flank, with better chances of success."[23]

With General Lee now persuaded to make the main Confederate assault on his right flank and not on his left, Lee said to General Ewell: "Then perhaps I had better draw you around toward my right, as the line will be very long and thin if you remain here, and the enemy may come down and break through it?" General Early was again the first to reject Lee's idea and reassured him: "[You] need not fear that the enemy would break through our line, and that we could repulse any force he could send against us." General Lee heard all he needed to hear. He would make an attack on his right tomorrow with the use of Longstreet's Corps and make an assault on his lift in conjunction.

Just after saddling up to depart from the meeting, Lee stated: "Longstreet is a very good fighter when he gets in position and gets everything ready, but he is so slow." Ewell was then ordered to create a diversion in the early morning to pull away Federal supports from the enemy center, but to also be ready to convert the diversion into a real attack if the situation warranted.[24]

The spirits of General Ewell and his brigade commanders were high. They had achieved a great victory this day by driving the enemy from the field and found themselves on good ground for tomorrow's attack. Furthermore, they had made convincing arguments, which had changed General Lee's mind to make the main assault on the right flank than on the left.

General Lee was not the type of leader who thought that since he was in command, his decision trumped all. He listened to his corps commanders and all his officers and did his best try to look at everything on the field of battle from the perspective of everyone and then arrive decisively at a decision. On this night, however, Lee's mind had still not yet been completely made up as to the attack plans for tomorrow. Colonel Charles Marshall of General Lee's staff came to Ewell shortly after Lee left and told Ewell of Lee's new order for Ewell to pull away from the town and make a complete assault on the enemy left flank and to not set up a diversion on the right flank. In his new orders, Lee stated: "I have not decided to fight here—and may probably draw off by my right flank along the heights ... which I understand offer many strong positions for us—so as to get between the enemy and Washington and Baltimore—and force them to attack us in position."[25]

The reconnaissance mission that Turner and Early had made earlier was still fresh within the mind of Ewell. Ewell saddled up and rode with Marshall to find Lee to try to argue his point yet again. Lee and Ewell talked for some time, with Ewell expressing his support for an attack on Culp's Hill. According to Ewell, the hill was unoccupied by the enemy. General Lee again reconsidered his orders and agreed, once again, to allow Ewell's Corps to stay in their current position and make plans for a diversionary attack on the Confederate left flank in the morning.

After arriving back at camp, Lieutenant Turner was awakened by General Ewell sometime after 2 a.m. and was ordered to ride to General Johnson's headquarters to suspend all plans to attempt to take Culp's Hill. General Lee, it turned out, had also "determined to suspend all offensive operations until Gen. Longstreet's arrival which was momentarily expected."[26]

After Turner had delivered the orders, Johnson confessed to him that he had already advanced on the hill with a small force and found that the enemy had already begun to occupy the hill. Johnson's men were fired upon by the 7th Indiana Infantry Regiment of General Cutler's Brigade and had been repulsed. Johnson also mentioned that a Federal courier had been intercepted with a dispatch from General Sykes of the Fifth Corps to General Hancock. In this dispatch, it was revealed that the Fifth Corps would come into position near Gettysburg about 2 a.m.

The find struck nerves throughout the Confederate commanders. They were still without Stuart and his experienced cavalry to give them any information as to the whereabouts of the Federal Army. Now it had been revealed that several Federal Corps were on the move and within a short distance of Gettysburg. The Confederates now knew that they would have a large fight on their hands the next morning.[27]

In the buildings and fields around Gettysburg, night cast eerie shadows across the barren landscape. The dead lay with the wounded and the groans sent chills down the most cold-hearted soldier's spine. In the Edward McPherson barn, Colonel Stone was among the wounded there and no surgeon had yet been found. Lieutenant R. B. Beath of the 88th Pennsylvania Infantry Regiment said he found the barn "full of bleeding and mangled soldiers in a most distressed and sickening condition ... their festering wounds and bind up their splintered bones. Many of the unfortunates were so shockingly lacerated that they were unable to move, being in some cases glued to the floor by the blood flowing from their gaping wounds congealed in pools under them..."[28]

Houses, churches, and buildings of all types were used to house the wounded. From John Burns' home to the Adams County Courthouse, the wounded were literally everywhere. One visitor to the field of battle recalled:

> [The courthouse was] in the very heart of Gettysburgh [*sic.*], we found our own soldiers lying on the bare floor, covered with blood, and dirt,

> and vermin, entirely naked having perhaps only a newspaper to protect their festering wounds from the flies!... Some of them were disfigured beyond the possibility of recognition. Oh! it is impossible to describe these mangled and marred fragments of humanity. One we saw with a great cavern in his side, from which the lungs protruded several inches. Another unfortunate, whose eyes had been shot out whilst trying to creep over a fence for shelter, was struck in the body five times![29]

Catherine Garlach, who had been protecting General Schimmelfennig at her home on Baltimore Street, had taken the general upstairs for safe keeping. Soon after she had done so, a Confederate soldier pushed open her front door and began to climb the stairs. As the soldier passed her on the steps, Catherine caught him by his coat and asked him what he was doing. The soldier replied with a shocked expression that he was going to use the house as a sharpshooter's nest. She stated: "You can't go up there, you will draw fire on this house full of defenseless women and children." The soldier left and Schimmelfennig eluded capture once again.[30]

While the town was busy attempting to care for the wounded, troops on both sides already on the battlefield and in town tried to get as much rest as possible. The fighting was sure to continue in the morning as other Federal and Confederate troops pressed forward all night to get to Gettysburg as soon as possible. The question on everyone's mind was what was the morning sunrise going to bring and would they live to see another one.

10
Conclusion

John B. Bachelder, one of the first great historians of the Battle of Gettysburg, stated:

> There is no question but what a combined attack on Cemetery Hill made within an hour, would have been successful. At the end of an hour the troops had been rallied, occupied strong positions, were covered by stone walls, and under the command and magnetic influence of General Hancock ... they would have held the position against any attack from the troops then up.[1]

In conclusion, even taking a brief walk around the fields and woodlots of Gettysburg gives the spectator a different outlook to what a battlefield actually is. Gettysburg ended the first day with a Confederate victory, a stalemate on the second, and a Federal victory on the third. The first day set the foundation as to what would become the bloodiest battle in the Civil War, resulting in approximately 51,000 casualties. The ground would forever be scarred and hallowed because of the deeds these men did here, and the sacrifices they paid can still be felt throughout the battlefield.

Many of the men lay on the field of battle after the first day. Some of them, knowing death was very near, thought of home. Others thought of sweethearts, families, children, fathers, mothers—they thought of what could have been and what was sadly coming. While animosities remained throughout the remainder of the war on both sides of the same nation, Confederate soldier Isaac G. Bradwell of the 31st Georgia Infantry Regiment recalled:

> The Federals fought no better at Gettysburg than they did anywhere else, but their splendid position won for them a victory where valor did not count. Where they fought in the open country the first day, it was like First and Second Manassas, the Wilderness, and wherever they met us in the open field...

He then spoke about his own troops: "Their steady courage, animated and enthused by their defiant yell, and the deadly accuracy of their fire will always break any line not well protected by earthworks or other obstacles too formidable to overcome..."[2]

After the first day, both armies had already taken on a different look. Huge losses, on both sides, would forever stagger the ranks, exposing the troops to the horrors of what had happened and what was yet to happen, and yet each one of them possessing as much courage as the next to still stand in line of battle against a foe that had only one purpose—to destroy them.

When night finally fell on July 1, the Federals had held the high ground. They had taken possession of Culp's Hill, the Round Tops, and Devil's Den and extended their line much farther to the left than the Confederates realized. Even while eventually being pushed back, the plans of General Buford and General Reynolds had succeeded when their troops had fallen back toward the high ground. Both General Meade and General Lee now had to decide how they wanted to continue the battle and either take an offensive or defensive approach. They also had to decide of what was best for their army: to stay on the fields of Gettysburg or retreat and surrender the battlefield to the enemy.

It is the opinion of the author that the true mettle of a soldier can be found throughout their writings and speeches. With that being said, around midnight of July 1–2, 1863, Colonel Strong Vincent was marching towards the sound of battle and arrived on the fields of nearby Hanover late that night. Vincent was a Pennsylvania native and, like Reynolds, was taking the invasion of his home state seriously. He ordered the old 83rd Pennsylvania's flag to be unfurled and brought the banner to the front of the brigade. The moonlight gleamed off the flag staff presenting an impressive spectacle. Vincent took his hat off and said, "What death more glorious can any man desire, than to die on the soil of old Pennsylvania, fighting for that flag?" Less than eighteen hours later, Vincent's blood would too be spilt while defending his home state like so many other boys in blue.[3]

Endnotes

Chapter 1

1. Kane to Rothermel, (March 21, 1874), Rothermel Papers, PSA.

Chapter 2

1. "Emancipation Proclamation," www.archives.gov; Alexander, E. P., *Fighting for the Confederacy*, p. 222.
2. Alexander, *Military Memoirs of a Confederate* (1907); Lee, F., *General Lee: A Biography of Robert E. Lee* (Charles River Editors) p. 186; Sten, J., *A Life of Gen. Robert E. Lee* (1876).
3. Fremantle, Sir A. J. L., *Three Months in the Southern States: April–June, 1863* (W. Blackwood and sons, 1863), p. 253.
4. Alexander, *Military Memoirs of a Confederate* (1907); Lee, *General Lee: A Biography of Robert E. Lee* (Charles River Editors) p. 186; Sten, *A Life of Gen. Robert E. Lee* (1876); Jones, W. J., *Personal Reminiscences, Anecdotes, and Letters of Gen. Robert E. Lee* (D. Appleton and Company, 1874); *The Century*, Vol. 35, (1888), p. 904.
5. "The Rebel Gen. Lee," *The New York Times* (August 1861).
6. *History of the 121st Pennsylvania*, p. 225; Taylor, *Four Years with General Lee*, p. 94; *Congressional Serial Set*, (1891), p. 88; *The War of the Rebellion*, Vols 1 53, (1889), pp. 881–82.
7. Barnhart, L. D., *The Reminiscences of Lorenzo D. Barnhart Co. B 110 Ohio*, Transcribed by Roger Barnhart 1998, p. 33; Milroy O.R 272:43; Nye, W. S., *Here Come the Rebels!*, (Louisiana State University Press, 1965) pp. 97–98.
8. Early, J. A., *Lieutenant General Jubal Anderson Early, C.S.A.* (J.B. Lippincott, 1912), pp. 236–261; Hotchkiss, McDonald *Make Me a Map of the Valley: The Civil War Journal of Stonewall Jackson's Topographer*; Stevenson, J. H., *Boots and Saddles* (Patriot Publishing Company 1879), pp. 189–97.
9. *Harper's Magazine*, Vol. 27, (Harper & Brothers, 1863), p. 413.
10. Letters of Charles Blackford to his wife, Susan Blackford June 14, 1863.
11. Stevenson, *Boots and Saddles*, (Patriot Publishing Company 1879), pp. 189–97; Higginson, H. L., *Life and Letters of Henry Lee Higginson* (Atlantic Monthly Press, 1921), p. 195; Blackford to his wife (June 16) Susan Blackford, ed.
12. Crowninshield, B. W., *A History of the First Regiment of Massachusetts Cavalry Volunteers* (Houghton, Mifflin and Company, 1891), p. 157.
13. *Congressional Serial Set*, (1891), p. 280.

14. *United States Congressional Serial Set 2773*, p. 195; *Ibid.*, p. 224.
15. *Ibid.*, pp. 227–28.
16. *Ibid.*, pp. 244–45.
17. Baylor, *Bull Run to Bull Run* (B.F. Johnson Publishing Company, 1900), p. 149.
18. Donaldson, *Inside the Army of the Potomac*, p. 285.
19. John P. Sheahan to his Father, (June 23), Maine Historical Society.
20. Congressional series, (June 21–22, 1863), pp. 911–13; United States Congressional Serial Set, 2773, p. 244.
21. General William Pender to his wife (June 21, 1863).
22. Congressional Edition 2773, U.S. Government Printing 1891, p. 905.
23. *Belfords Magazine*, Vol. 6, (1891), p. 155; Congressional Edition 2773, p. 914.
24. Russell, C. W., *The memoirs of Colonel John S. Mosby* (Little, Brown, 1917) pp. 174–75.
25. SHSP, Vol. 37, (1909), p. 89; Fiebeger, G. J., *The campaign of Gettysburg*, p. 128; Congressional Edition 2773, (June 22, 1863), p. 915; *The Century Illustrated Monthly Magazine*, Vol. 34, (Century Company, 1887) p. 152.
26. Congressional edition 2773, p. 915; Congressional Serial Set, issue 2773, p. 261.
27. Congressional Serial Set, Issue 2773, (1891), p. 267; *The Civil War letters of William Dorsey Pender to Fanny Pender*, edited by William W. Hassler, (Chapel Hill; University of North Carolina Press, 1999).
28. *The Century Illustrated Monthly Magazine*, Vol. 34, (Century Company, 1887), p. 152; SHSP *Stuart's Cavalry in the Gettysburg Campaign*, p. 198.
29. Congressional Serial Set, p. 927; SHSP *Stuart's Cavalry in the Gettysburg Campaign*, p. 198.
30. Congressional Serial Set, (1891), p. 295.
31. *Ibid.*, pp. 195–97; McCellan, *The Life and Campaigns of Major-General J. E. B. Stuart* (Houghton, Mifflin, 1885), p. 322; Congressional Serial Set, (1891), p. 307.
32. *Ibid.*, p. 313.
33. *Ibid.*, p. 314; *Ibid.*, p. 317.
34. Ewell O.R; Early O.R.; Hoke, *The Great Invasion of 1863: or General Lee in Pennsylvania* (W.J Shuey, 1887), pp. 165–71.
35. Early, *Lieutenant General Jubal Anderson Early, C.S.A.* (J. B. Lippincott, 1912), p. 256.
36. *Ibid.*, p. 256; Pennypacker, *Historical and Biographical Sketches* (R.A. Triple, 1883), p. 341; Early O.R.; Jacobs, *Notes on the Rebel Invasion of Maryland and Pennsylvania* (J.B. Lippincott and Company, 1864), pp. 12–18; Myers, *The Comanches: A History of White's Battalion Virginia Cavalry* (Continental Book Company, 1871), p. 192; Pennypacker, pp. 341–42.
37. Pennypacker, p. 342.
38. Hoke, *The Great Invasion of 1863*, p. 171; *Ibid.*, p. 172, Early, *Lieutenant General Jubal Anderson Early, C.S.A.*, p. 258; Buehler, F. J., *Recollections of the Rebel Invasion and One Woman Experience During the Battle of Gettysburg* (Star and Sentinel Print, 1900), p. 11; Pennypacker, *Historical and Biographical Sketches*, pp. 343–344; Bates, Vol. 5, p. 1225; Early, p. 257.
39. Pennypacker, S. W., *Pennsylvania in American History* (W.J. Campbell, 1910), pp. 384–95; Pennypacker, *26th Pennsylvania Emergency Infantry*, pp. 6–11; Prowell, G. R., *History of York Country, Pennsylvania, Vol. 1* (J.H. Beers, 1907), p. 404; Early, *Lieutenant General Jubal Anderson Early*, p. 257; Wiley, E., *The United States, Vol 5.* (American Educational Alliance, 1909), p. 251; Jacovs, *Notes on the Rebel Invasion of Maryland and Pennsylvania*, pp. 15–22.

40. Hoke, *The Great Invasion of 1863*, p. 173; Buehler, *Recollections of the Rebel Invasion and One Woman's Experience During the Battle of Gettysburg* (Gettysburg, 1900), p. 11.
41. Hoke, *The Great Invasion of 1863*, p. 184.
42. Alexander, *Fighting for the Confederacy*, p. 228–29.
43. United States Congressional Serial Set 2773, p. 336.
44. *Ibid.*, p. 349; *Ibid.*, p. 352.
45. *Ibid.*, p. 370; Early, *Lieutenant General Jubal Anderson Early C.S.A.*, pp. 258–59.
46. Congressional Edition, Vol. 2773, pp. 942–43.
47. Congressional Serial Set, p. 370.
48. U.S. Congressional 2773, pp. 373–74.
49. *The Christian Advocate, Vol. 89* (Hunt & Eaton,1914), p. 917.
50. Gilbert, J., *The Century Illustrated Monthly Magazine*, Vol. 86, (Scriber and Company, The Century Company, 1913), p. 9; U.S. Congressional 2773, p. 374.
51. Hoke, *The Great Invasion of 1863*, p. 183; Early, *Lieutenant General Jubal Anderson Early, C.S.A.*, p. 259.
52. Stiles, R., *Four Yearts Under Marse Robert* (1904), p. 203.
53. *Ibid.*, p. 205.
54. Hoke, *The Great Invasion of 1863*, p. 184; Moore, F., *The Rebellion Record, a Diary of American Events* (G.P. Putnam, 1864), p. 328.
55. Gordon, J. B., *Reminiscences of the Civil War* (C. Scribner's Sons, 1903), pp. 143–44.
56. Early, *Lieutenant General Jubal Anderson Early, C.S.A.*, pp. 259–60.
57. *Confederate Veteran*, Vol. 27, (1919) pp. 300–01.
58. Gordon, *Reminiscences of the Civil War*, pp. 147–50.
59. *Confederate Veteran*, Vol. 27, (1919) pp. 300–01.
60. Gordon, *Reminiscences of the Civil War*, pp. 146–48.
61. *Ibid.*, p. 150.
62. Early O.R.; Early, *Lieutenant General Jubal Anderson Early, C.S.A.*, p. 261.
63. Early, *Lieutenant General Jubal Anderson Early*, p. 261; U.S. Congressional Series 2773, pp. 375–78.
64. General Ewell to Lizzie (wife); Ewell Letters.
65. Sorrel, G. M., *Recollections of a Confederate Staff Officer* (The Neale Publishing Company, 1905), p. 164.
66. *Ibid.*
67. *United Service*, (1896), p. 101.
68. Pender letters to his Fanny Pender.
69. Wainwright, C., *A Diary of Battle*, p. 228.
70. SHSP Vols 22–24, p. 17; *Ibid.*, p. 258; Sorrel, *Recollections of a Confederate Staff Officer*, p. 165.
71. Congressional Serial Set, 1891, p. 397.
72. U.S. Congressional 2773, p. 400.
73. *The Independent*, Vol. 74 (Independent Corporation, 1913), p. 1109; *Ibid.*, p. 402; E.D. Burdock Diary, (Chicago Historical Society); Meade, *Life and Letters of George Gordon Meade* (C. Scribner's Sons, 1913), p. 74.
74. U.S. Congressional 2773, p. 414.
75. Curtis, O. B., *History of the Twenty-fourth Michigan of the Iron Brigade, known as theDetroit and Wayne County Regiment* (Winn & Hammond, 1891), p. 423.
76. *Ibid.*, p. 415; Hoke, *The Great Invasion of 1863*, p. 560.
77. Congressional Serial 2773, pp. 416–20.
78. *The United States*, Vol. 5, p. 253.

79. *The War of the Rebellion*, Vol. 27, Part 3, (1889), p. 418.
80. *Annals of the War* (Times Publishing Company, 1879), pp. 208–09.
81. U.S. Congressional 2773, p. 422.
82. *Ibid.*, pp. 420–25.
83. *Congressional Series of United States Public Documents*, (U.S. Government Printing Office, 1865), p. 351.
84. Hoke, *Historical Reminiscences of the War* (M.A. Foltz, 1884), p. 69; *Annals of the War*, pp. 419–20; Alexander, *Fighting for the Confederacy*, pp. 229–30.
85. Dawes, R. D., *Service with the Sixth Wisconsin Volunteers* (E.R. Alderman and Sons, 1890), p. 158.
86. Early, *Lieutenant General Jubal Anderson Early*, p. 265.
87. Porter, *Fighting for the Confederacy*, p. 230.
88. Sypher, J. R., *History of the Pennsylvania Reserve Corps* (Elias Barr and Company, 1865); *History of the 121st Regiment Pennsylvania Volunteers* (Press of Catholic standards and times, 1906), pp. 215–16.
89. *History of the 121st Regiment Pennsylvania Volunteers*, p. 216; Howard, O. O., *Campaign and Battle of Gettysburg* (Atlantic Monthly 38, 1876), pp. 52–53; *Journal of the United States Cavalry Association, Vol. 8*, (1895), pp. 178–79; Buford, *A Genealogy of the Buford Family in America*, (1903), p. 218.
90. Congressional Serial Set, (1891), p. 924.
91. SHSP, (1877), p. 157.

Chapter 3

1. *Confederate Veteran*, Vol. 14, (S.a. Cunningham, 1906), p. 308.
2. The National Tribune, *The First Shot At Gettysburg*, October 30, 1902; *Opened the Fight at Gettysburg.*
3. *Ibid.*, p. 308.
4. *The History of the Fighting Fourteenth* (1911), p. 81; Hoke, *Historical Reminiscences of the War*, p. 70; Marye, *The First Gun at Gettysburg* (1895), p. 30; 8th Illinois Cavalry, *Biography written by Lt. Col. Jesse Martinez*; Hard, A., *History of the Eighth Cavalry Regiment, Illinois Volunteers, During the Great Rebellion* (1868), p. 256; Public Domain.
5. *The American Historical Register*, Vol. 12, (1895), p. 229; *Annual Reunion of Pegram Battalion Association* (1886), p. 15; SHSP, Vol. 14, p. 16.
6. *The American Historical Register and Monthly Gazette of the Historic, military and Patriotic-Hereditary Societies of the United States of America*, Vol. 2 (1895), p. 1229.
7. Andrews, C. H., *Condensed History of the 3rd Georgia Volunteer Infantry* (Georgia Archives, 1885).
8. Hard, *History of the Eighth Cavalry Regiment, Illinois Volunteers, During the Great Rebellion*, pp. 256–59.
9. *Ibid.*
10. Moon, W. H., "Beginning of the Battle at Gettysburg," *Confederate Veteran*, Vol. 33, (1925), pp. 449–50.
11. Barnett, B., *Confederate Artillery operations on the First Day of Gettysburg*, pp. 200–02; Hoke, *The Great Invasion of 1863*, p. 259; *Annals of War*, p. 307; Wainwright, *A Diary of Battle*, p. 232.
12. Moon, "Beginning of the Battle at Gettysburg," *Confederate Veteran*, Vol. 33, (1935), p. 450.

13. Hard, *History of the Eighth Cavalry Regiment, Illinois Volunteers*, pp. 256–57; Weld, *War Diary and letters of Stephen Minot Weld* (Cornell University Library), p. 229; Lt. Veil to McConaughy, (April 7, 1864, McConaughy Collections, Gettysburg College); Wainwright, *A Diary of Battle*, pp. 232–34.
14. *Ibid.*; Wainwright, *A Diary of Battle*, pp. 232–34; *History of the 121st Pennsylvania Volunteers*, p. 221; Congressional Edition, Vol. 2771, (1891), p. 924.
15. Jerome to Hancock, *Bachelder Papers* (Oct. 1865) Vol. 1, p. 201; Church, *The Galaxy, Vol.* 22, (1876), p. 154.
16. *Ibid.*, p. 827; Hard, *History of the Eight Illinois Cavalry*, p. 257; Weld, *War Diary and Letters of Stephen Minot Weld*, pp. 229–32.
17. Huntington, *8th New York Cavalry* (Palmyra New York, 1902), p. 14.
18. Lt Veil to McConaughy, (April 7, 1864), Mcconaughy Collection, Gettysburg College.
19. Congressional Serial Set (1891), p. 948.
20. Wainwright, *A Diary of Battle.*
21. Dawes, *Service with the Sixth Wisconsin, Volunteers* (E.R. Alderman and Sons, 1890), p. 164.
22. *Ibid.*, p. 164.
23. Johnson, *Battles and Leaders of the Civil War, Vol. 3*, p. 108; Hard, *History of the Eight Cavalry Regiment, Illinois*, p. 257.
24. Report of the Twenty- fourth Annual Re-union at Boston, Mass, (June 27 and 28, 1893), p. 14.

Chapter 4

1. Veil to McConaughy, (April 7, 1864).
2. *Ibid.*, p. 164–66.
3. *Ibid.*; *The United States Army and Navy Journal and Gazette of Regular and Volunteer forces, Vol. 4* (June 22, 1867), p. 695; Bates, S. P., *Martial Deed of Pennsylvania* (T.H. Davis and Company, 1876), pp. 471–74.
4. Wainwright, *Diary of Battle*, pp. 142–52.
5. *Confederate Veteran*, Vol. 14, (1906), p. 308.
6. Bird, W., *Stories of the Civil War Company C, 13th Regiment of Alabama Volunteers* (Advocate Press, 1900), pp. 6–9.
7. *Ibid.*
8. Johnson, R. U., *Battles and Leaders of the Civil War, Vol. 3, Part 1* (Century, 1888), p. 285.
9. Henry Heth O.R.
10. Congressional Serial Set, p. 964.
11. p. 265; Congressional Edition, 2772, p. 111; *Glimpses of the Nation's Struggle* (1899) pp. 340–41; Congressional Edition 2772, p. 637; *Ibid.*, pp. 648–49; Weld, *War Diary and letters of Stephen M. Weld*, p. 232; Leander G. Woolard Diary, (Memphis State University).
12. *Ibid.*, Woolard Diary.
13. Stine, J. H., *A History of the Army of the Potomac* (J.B. Rodgers Printing Company, 1892), p. 463; Mississippi Valley Collections; *The War of the Rebellion* (1889), pp. 251–54; Dawes, *Service with the Sixth Wisconsin Volunteers*, p. 166; Congressional Edition 2772, p. 649; Leander G. Woolard Diary, (Mississippi Valley Collections, July 1, 1863); *Publications of the Mississippi Historical Society, Vol. 9*, (Mississippi Historical Society, 1906), p. 30.

14. Congressional Serial Set, (1891), p. 253.
15. Hurd, D. H., *History of Otsego Country, New York* (Everts & Fariss, 1878), p. 61; Evans, C. A., *Confederate Military History* (Confederate Publishing Company, 1899), p. 174.
16. United Congressional Series, 2771, p. 282; J.V. Pierce to Bachelder, (Sept. 6, 1880–April, 1886).
17. *Ibid.*; *Final Report on the Battlefield of Gettysburg* (J.B. Lyon Company, 1902), pp. 990–995.
18. J.V. Pierce to Bachelder, (Sept. 6, 1880–April, 1886).
19. *Ibid.*; Sine, *A History of the Army of the Potomac*, p. 463; Congressional Edition, 2772, p. 649.
20. J.V. Pierce to Bachelder, (Sept. 6, 1880–April, 1886).
21. *Ibid.*; *War Talks in Kansas Volume 1* (Press of the F. Hudson Publishing Company, 1906), p. 280.
22. United States Congressional, 2771, p. 282.
23. Halls O.R.; Congressional Edition, 2772, p. 649; United States Congressional Series Set Issue 2771, (1891), pp. 350–56.
24. *Ibid.*, p. 355.
25. SHSP, (1880) p. 321.
26. Congressional serial set, (1865), p. 403.
27. Weld, *War Diary and Letters of Stephen Minot Weld*, p. 232; Congressional series of United States public documents, (1865), p. 404.
28. Weld, *War Diary and Letters of Stephen M. Weld*, pp. 228–35.
29. Weld, *War Diary and Letters of Stephen M. Weld*, p. 232; Meade O.R.
30. Congressional Serial Set, (1865), p. 487; Congressional Serial Set (1891), p. 458; Mosby, J. S., *Stuart's Cavalry in the Gettysburg Campaign* (Moffat Yard, 1908), p. 186; Charles H. Morgan to Bachelder, Vol. 3, pp. 1350–53; Walker, F. A., *History of the Second Army Corps in the Army of the Potomac*, Vol. 2, part 4 (C. Scribner's Sons, 1891), p. 264.
31. *Ibid.*; Dawes, *Service with the Wisconsin Volunteers*, p. 164; *Confederate Veteran*, Vol. 20, (S.A. Cunningham, 1912), p. 439.
32. United States Congressional Serial Set 1212, (U.S. Government Printing office, 1865), pp. 422–23.

Chapter 5

1. Dawes O.R.; Dawes, *Service with the Sixth Wisconsin Volunteers*, pp. 166–68.
2. W.B. Murphy June 29, 1900, Bragg Papers, State Historical Society of Wisconsin.
3. Dawes, *Service with the Sixth Wisconsin Volunteers*, pp. 166–68.
4. Dawes, *Service with the Sixth Wisconsin Volunteers*, p. 169.
5. *Ibid.*, pp. 161–62.
6. Fowler O.R.; Pye O.R.
7. Dawes, *Service with the Sixth Wisconsin Volunteers*, pp. 162–171; *The Cyclopedic Review of Current History, Vol. 6* (Evening News Association, 1896), p. 240; Public Domain; Congressional 2772, p. 637.
8. *Glimpses of the Nations Struggle*, p. 344; Lee, A. E., *The Battle of Gettysburg* (A.H. Smythe, 1888), pp. 109–10; Vanderslice, J. M., *Gettysburg: Where and How the Regiments Fought and Troops they Encountered* (Philadelphia, 1897), pp. 41–42.
9. Howard O.R.; Howard, *Autobiography of Oliver Otis Howard, Major General, United States Army* (The Baker and Taylor Company, 1907), pp. 409–11.

10. *Ibid.*, p. 410.
11. *Ibid.*, pp. 411–414.
12. *Ibid.*
13. Howard O.R.; Howard, *Autobiography of Oliver Otis Howard, Major General, United States Army* (The Baker and Taylor Company, 1907), pp. 410–14.
14. Howard O.R.; Howard, *Autobiography of Oliver Otis Howard, Major General, United States Army*, p. 413; *Ibid.*; Weld, *War Diaries and Letters of Stephen M. Weld*, p. 233; Burrage, H. S., *Gettysburg and Lincoln* (G.P. Putnam's Sons, 1906), p. 19.
15. J. W. M. Jones, SHSP, (1877), p. 126.
16. Longstreet, *From Manassas to Appomattox* (J.B. Lippincott Company, 1903), pp. 351–52; Taylor, W. H., *Four Years with General Lee* (Chamberlayne Appleton, 1878), pp. 92–93.
17. SHSP, (1878), p. 60.
18. *The Annals of the War*, (1879), p. 307; Young, J. B., *The Battle of Gettysburg* (Harper, 1913), p. 138; Brown, C., *Campbell Brown's Civil War*, pp. 204–05.
19. *Ibid.*, p. 205.
20. Report of the Joint Committee on the Conduct of the War of the Second Session, p. 403.
21. Wade, B. F., *Army of the Potomac, Congress Joint Committee*, pp. 485–86.
22. Welles, G., *Diary of Gideon Welles, Vol. 1*, (1911), p. 352.
23. Report of the Joint Committee on the Conduct of the War, (1865), p. 827.

Chapter 6

1. Walker, *History of the Second Army Corps in the Army of the Potomac*, pp. 265–66; Hinkley, J. W., *A Narrative of Service with the Third Wisconsin Infantry* (Wisconsin History Commission, 1912), p. 82.
2. *Confederate Veteran*, Vol. 5; SHSP (1876), p. 148.
3. Congressional Serial Set, (1865), p. 116; Baxter O.R.; Rodes O.R.
4. Rodes O.R.; *History of the 121st Pennsylvania*, p. 225.
5. Thompson, J. M., *Reminiscences of the Autausa Rifles* (Autaugaville, Alabama, 1879), p. 7.
6. Rodes O.R.
7. Taylor, *Four Years with General Lee*, p. 94.
8. Brown, *Campbell Brown's Civil War*, p. 205; Ewells O.R.; Rodes O.R.
9. O'Neal O.R.; SHSP, (1877) p. 158.
10. Rodes O.R.
11. SHSP Vols 1–2, (1891), p. 147.
12. *Histories of Several Regiments and Battalions from North Carolina in the Great War*, Vol. 3, p. 634; *Ibid.*, Rodes.
13. *Histories of Several Regiments and Battalions from North Carolina in the Great War*, Vol. 1, p. 634; SHSP, (1897) pp. 12–14.
14. *Ibid.*, p. 13.
15. *Ibid.*, pp. 13–14.
16. Rodes O.R.
17. Rodes O.R.; Coffin, C. C., *The boys of '61* (Estes and Laurel, 1885), p. 272.
18. *Ibid.*, pp. 272–73.
19. Davis, C., *Three Years in the Army: The story of the Thirteenth Massachusetts Volunteers from July 16, 1861, to August 1, 1864* (Estes and Lauriat, 1894), p. 244.

20. SHSP, (Jan 26–Jan 27, 1864) Park War Diary; Coffin, *Four Years of Fighting* (1866), p. 272; Baxter O.R.; Robinson's O.R; Doubleday, A., *Chancellorsville and Gettysburg, Vol. 6* (C. Scribner's Sons, 1882), p. 143; Clark, *Histories of Several Regiments and Battalions from North Carolina in the Great War, Vol. 2*, p. 235.
21. *Glimpses of the Nations Struggle, Vol. 5* (1908), p. 49; *Ibid.*, p. 635; *Ibid.*, Vol. 2, p. 236; Doubleday, p. 143; *Histories of Several Regiments and Battalions*, p. 237; Vautier, J., *History of the 88th Pennsylvnia Volunteers in the War for the Union* (J.B. Lippincott Company, 1894), pp. 103–110.
22. Vautier, *History of the 88th Pennsylvania Volunteers in the War for the Union, 1861–1865* (1894), pp. 130–35; Clark, *Histories of Several Regiments and Battalions from North Carolina in the Great War, Vol. 12*, p. 238.
23. Vautier, *History of the 88th Pennsylvania Volunteers in the War for the Union, 1861–1865* (1894), p. 135.
24. *Glimpses of the Nations Struggle*, pp. 50–51.
25. *Histories of Several Regiments and Battalions from North Carolina in the Great War, Vol. 2*, p. 149.
26. Small, A., *The Road to Richmond*, pp. 101–22; Douglas Southall Freeman papers; Vautier, *History of the 88th Pennsylvania Volunteers in the War for the Union* (J.B Lippincott Company, 1894), pp. 106–07.
27. *Histories of Several Regiments and Battalions from North Carolina in the Great War, Vol. 3*, p. 119; Rodes O.R.
28. *Ibid.*, p. 151; Rodes O.R.; *Histories of Several Regiments and Battalions from North Carolina in the Great War, Vol. 1*, p. 637; Ewell O.R.
29. Ewells O.R.; *Histories of Several...*, p. 237; Berkeley, H. R., *Four Years in the Confederate Artillery* (Virginia Historical Society), p. 50.
30. Charles C. Blackhall memoir.
31. *Glimpses of the Nations Struggle, Vol. 5*, pp. 50–51; Small, *The Road to Richmond*, pp. 98–99.
32. *Glimpses of the Nations Struggle, Vol. 5*, p. 51.
33. Small, *The Road to Richmond*, p. 99.
34. *Ibid.*
35. Kimball, W., *The 13th Massachusetts at Gettysburg* (National Tribune, May 14, 1886); Letter of Major H. J. Shaeffer (Lebanon Courier, July 23, 1863) file in Gettysburg National Military Park Library.
36. *Several Histories of Regimental...Vol. 2*, pp. 525–26.
37. Rodes O.R.; Clark, *20th Regiment of North Carolina, Vol. 12*, p. 238.
38. Hunter, R., *Sketches of War History, 1861-1865: Papers Read Before the Ohio Commandery of the Military Order of the Loyal Legion of the United States, Vol. 4* (R. Clarke & Company, 1896), p. 185.
39. Jones, SHSP, (1880), p. 87; Daniel O.R.
40. *Ibid.*; Daniel O.R.
41. Stones O.R.; SHSP, Vol. 37, (1909), pp. 266–69.
42. *Ibid.*, p. 268.
43. Wainwright, *A Diary of Battle*, pp. 230–235.
44. Underwood, *Battle and Leaders of the Civil War*, p. 285.
45. Mudge, A., *A History of the Class of 1854 in Dartmouth College* (Dartmouth College, 1898), p. 74; Doubleday, O.R.
46. Colonel Roy Stone O.R.; Brockett, L. P., *The Camp* (1866), p. 503.
47. *Ibid.*; Stine, *History of the Army of the Potomac* (1897), p. 477; Hunter, R., *Sketches of War History, Vol. 4* (B. Clark and Co., 1896), pp. 184–185.

48. Livermore, M., *My Story of the War: A Woman's Narrative of Four Years Personal Experience as Nurse in the Union Army* (A.D. Worthington, 1890), pp. 42–44.
49. Congressional Serial Set, (1891), p. 342.
50. Moore, F., *A Rebellion Record* (G.P. Putnam, 1864), p. 50; Stones O.R.; SHSP Vol. 37; Dwight O.R.
51. SHSP, Vol. 37, pp. 255–282.
52. Fremantle, pp. 254–55; *Avery Harris Civil War Journal* (Luzerne, Pa: Luzerne National Bank, 2000), pp. 64–65.
53. *Ibid.*, p. 237.
54. *The War of the Rebellion*, Vols 1–55, pp. 322–25; Thorp's Account, *Histories of Several Regiments...*, Vol. 3, p. 89.
55. *Ibid.*, Vol. 2, pp. 351–52.
56. *Ibid.*, p. 352.
57. *The War of the Rebellion* (U.S. Government Printing Office, 1889), p. 323.
58. Edwin Gearhart account, March 19, 1900; *The War of the Rebellion* (U.S. Government Printing Office, 1889), p. 327; Warren, H. N., *Two Reunions of the 142nd Regiment, Pa Vols* (Courier Company, printer, 1890), p. 22.
59. Downey, J. W., *A Lethal Tour of Duty: A history of the 142d Regiment Pennsylvania Voluntary Infantry, 1862–65*, pp. 31–32
60. Balsley, J. R., *A Gettysburg Reminiscence* (National Tribune, May 19, 1898).
61. *The War of the Rebellion* (U.S. Government Printing Office, 1889), p. 327; McFarland O.R.
62. *Confederate Veteran*, Vol. 25 (1917), p. 354.
63. *The War of the Rebellion*, p. 327; *Confederate Veteran*, Vol. 17, p. 110; Evans, C. A., *Confederate Military History: A Library of Confederate States History, Vol. 4* (Confederate Publishing Company, 1899), p. 414; John R. Lane Interview, W. H. S Burgwyn Papers, (North Carolina Department of Archives and History).
64. *Ibid.*, p. 942.
65. McFarland O.R
66. *The Charlotte Observer* from Charlotte, North Carolina (Sunday, July 15, 1900), p. 9.
67. Congressional Serial Set, (1891), p. 643, Jones account.
68. Addresses Delivered Before the Confederate Veterans Association of Savannah, Ga, (The Association, 1912), pp. 36–37; Congressional Series, 2771, p. 189; Memoirs of Henry Heth.

Chapter 7

1. Howard, *Autobiography of Oliver Otis Howard*, pp. 416–17.
2. *Confederate Veteran*, Vol. 26, p. 162; Lee, *The Battle of Gettysburg*, p. 110; Early, *Lieutenant General Jubal Anderson Early...*, p. 267.
3. *Confederate Veteran*, Vol. 26, (S.A. Cunningham, 1918), p. 162; Stiles, *Four Years Under Marse Robert*, (1904), p. 211.
4. Congressional Serial Set, (1891), p. 729.
5. *Ibid.*
6. *Confederate Veteran*, Vol. 26, (1918), p. 162.
7. Kiefer, W. R., *History of the One Hundred and Fifty-Third Regiment Pennsylvania Volunteer Infantry* (Chemical Publishing Company, 1909), pp. 211–12.
8. *Ibid.*, p. 212.

9. *Ibid.*, p. 213.
10. *Ibid.*, pp. 213–15.
11. *Bachelder Papers*, Vol. 2, pp. 744–45.
12. *Ibid.*, p. 745.
13. Barlow letter to his mother; SHSP, Vols 21–22, (1893), pp. 338–39.
14. *Ibid.*, p. 339; *Putnam's Magazine*, Vol. 4, (G.P. Putnam and Sons, 1869), pp. 319–22; *Confederate Veteran* Magazine (April, 1923).
15. Johnson, R. U., *Battles and leaders of the Civil War*, Vol. 3, (1888), p. 281.
16. *Confederate Veteran* (S.A. Cunningham, 1897), p. 614.
17. Applegate, J., *Reminiscences and Letters of George Arrowsmith of New Jersey* (John H. Cook Publisher, 1893), pp. 216–20.
18. *Confederate Veteran*, Vol. 31 (April, 1923), p. 138.
19. *Putnam's Magazine*, Vol. 4, (G.P. Putnam and Sons, 1869), pp. 319–22.
20. *Ibid.*, p. 322.
21. Knott, K., *The Southern Bivouac* (1886), p. 441.
22. Applegate, *Reminiscences and Letters of George Arrowsmith of New Jersey*, p. 216.
23. *Ibid.*, p. 217.
24. Trautmann, F., *Twenty Months in Captivity: memoirs of a Union Officer in Confederate Prisons* (Fairleigh Dickinson University Press, 1987), pp. 27–29.
25. Congressional Serial Set, (1891), p. 755.
26. George Mason letter to his mother.

Chapter 8

1. Wainwright, *A Diary of Battle*, pp. 235–37.
2. Dawes, *Service with the Sixth Wisconsin Volunteers*, pp. 175–79; Dawes O.R.
3. *Ibid.*, p. 235.
4. Small, *The Road to Richmond*, p. 101; Caldwell, *The History of a Brigade of South Carolinians...*, p. 99; SHSP (1897), p. 259.
5. County, A., *Company K 14 South Carolina Volunteers*, pp. 19–20.
6. Caldwell, J. F. J., *The History of a Brigade of South Carolinians, known first as 'Greg's', and subsequently as 'McGowan's Brigade'* (King and Baird, 1866), pp. 97–98.
7. *Pennsylvania at Gettysburg* (W.S Ray, State Printer, 1914), p. 909; *Ibid.*
8. *Bachelder Papers*, September 6, 1880 to April 12, 1886, p. 903; *War of the Rebellion*, serial 43, p. 280; Brown, V. D., *A Colonel at Gettysburg and Spotsylvania* (The State Company, 1931), p. 79.
9. Dawes, *Service with the Sixth Wisconsin Volunteers*, p. 176.
10. *History of the 121st Regiment Pennsylvania Volunteers*, p. 56.
11. Wainwright, *A Diary of Battle*, p. 235.
12. *Ibid.*, pp. 236–37.
13. Small, *The Road to Richmond*, p. 101.
14. *Ibid.*, p. 102.
15. Schurz, C., *The Reminiscences of Carl Schurz*, pp. 14–15; *Ibid.*, 18–19.
16. *Recollections and Reminiscences of 1861–1865*; Congressional Series 2771, pp. 327–30.
17. *Confederate Veteran*, Vol. 5 (1897), p. 615.
18. Congressional Serial Set (1891), p. 607.

Chapter 9

1. Osborn, H., *Trials and Triumphs* (A.C. Mcclurg and Company, 1904), p. 285.
2. Shurz, *The Reminiscences of Carl Schurz*, p. 13.
3. *Ibid.*, p. 13; *Report of the Joint Committee on Conduct of War, Part 1*, p. 405; Johnson, *Battles and leaders of the Civil War*, p. 285.
4. *Ibid.*, p. 13; *Bachelder Papers*, Vol. 3, pp. 1351–52.
5. Congressional Serial Set, (1893), p. 584.
6. Ray, W. S., *Pennsylvania at Gettysburg* (State Printer, 1912), p. 626.
7. Congressional Serial Set, (1891), p. 696; Schurz, *The Reminiscences of Carl Schurz*, pp. 15–19.
8. Congressional Series of the United States Public Documents, Vol. 2772, (1891), p. 555; Early, *Lieutenant General Jubal Anderson Early, C.S.A.*, p. 269.
9. SHSP Vol. 43, (1920), p. 57.
10. Early, *Lieutenant General Jubal Anderson Early, C.S.A.*, p. 269; Brown, *Campbell Brown's Civil War*, p. 211.
11. SHSP (1878), p. 61; Taylor, W. H., *Four Years with General Lee* (1877), p. 95.
12. Longstreet, J., *From Manassas to Appomattox*, p. 358.
13. *Ibid.*, p. 358; SHSP, Vols 4–5, (1877), p. 61.
14. Longstreet, H. D., *Lee and Longstreet at High Tide*, (1904), pp. 37–39; Longstreet, *From Manassas to Appomattox*, pp. 355–40; *The United Service* Magazine, pp. 71–72.
15. SHSP, Vol. 43, (1920), p. 57.
16. SHSP, Vols 33–34, p. 145.
17. SHSP, Vol. 37, (1909), p. 120.
18. McDonald, W. N., *The Southern Bivouac*, (1886), p. 441.
19. SHSP (1877), p. 262.
20. J. A. Early Papers; SHSP, Vol. 43, (1920), p. 57; *The War of the Rebellion*, (1889), p. 496.
21. Applegate, p. 222; Turner, T., "Gettysburg, Captain Turner," *The United Service*, Vol. 115, (1897), p. 71.
22. Rev. Jones, SHSP (1877), pp. 270–75.
23. *Ibid.*, p. 272; Ewell's O.R.
24. *Ibid.*, pp. 272–74; Marshall to Early, (March, 23, 1870), Early Papers, Virginia Historical Society.
25. Brown, *Campbell Brown's Civil War*, p. 218.
26. Turner, T., *Gettysburg, Captain Turner*; Early Papers.
27. *Ibid.*
28. John Vaunter in *Philadelphia Weekly Press*, Vol. 15, (Nov. 10, 1886).
29. Stone, E. W., *Rhode Island in the Rebellion* (G.H. Whitney, 1864), p. 269.
30. Garlach Diary.

Chapter 10

1. Brock, SHSP, Vols 5–6, (1878), p. 172.
2. *Confederate Veteran*, Vol. 30, (1922) p. 429.
3. *History of Erie Country, Pennsylvania, Vol. 1*, (1884), p. 967.

Bibliography

Alexander, E. P., *Fighting of the Confederacy: The Personal Recollections of General Edward Porter Alexander* (UNC Press, 1998)

Andrews, C., *Condensed History of the 3rd Georgia Volunteer Infantry* (Georgia Archives, 1885)

Applegate, J., *Reminiscences and Letters of George Arrowsmith of New Jersey* (John H. Cook Publisher, 1893)

Barnett, B., *Confederate Artillery Operations on the First Day at Gettysburg* (National Park Service Gettysburg Seminar Papers, 2005)

Baylor, G., *Bull Run to Bull Run: or, Four Years in the Army of Northern Virginia. Containing a Detailed Account of the Career and Adventures of the Baylor Light Horse, Company B., Twelfth Virginia Cavalry, C.S.A* (B.F. Johnson Publishing Company, 1900)

Bennett, G. R., *Days of 'Uncertainty and Dread': The Ordeal Endured by the Citizens of Gettysburg* (G.R. Bennett, 1994)

Berkeley, H. R., *Four Years in the Confederate Artillery: the Diary of Private Henry Robinson Berkeley* (University of North Carolina Press, 1961)

Bird, W., *Stories of the Civil War, Company C, 13th Regiment of Alabama Volunteers* (Advocate Press, 1900)

Bliss, P., *Life and Letters of Henry Lee Higginson* (Read Books, 2007)

Breshears, G., *Major Granville Haller: Dismissed with Malice* (Heritage Books, 2006)

Brown, C., *Campbell Brown's Civil War: With Ewell and the Army of Northern Virginia* (LSU Press, 2004)

Bueller, F. J., *One Woman's Experience During the Battle of Gettysburg* (Star and Sentinel Print, 1896)

Barrage, H. S., *Gettysburg and Lincoln: The Battle, The Cemetery, and The National Park* (G.P. Putnam's Sons, 1906)

Brock, R., *Southern Historical Society Papers, Vol. 25* (1897)

Caldwell, J. F. J., *The History of a Brigade of South Carolinians Known First as Gregg's and Subsequently as 'McGowan's Brigade'* (King and Baird, 1866)

Chance, M., *Prelude to Invasion: Lee's Preparations and the Second Battle of Winchester* (Gettysburg Magazine, 1998)

Coco, G. A., *A Vast Sea of Misery: A History and Guide to the Union and Confederate Field Hospitals at Gettysburg, July–November 20, 1863* (Thomas Publications, 1988)

Coffin, C., *The Boys of '61 or, Four Years of Fighting* (Boston: Estes and Luriat, 1885)

Collins, T., *Robert E. Lee: The Story of the Great Confederate General* (Capstone, 2011)

Cooke, J. E., *A Life of Gen. Robert E. Lee* (D. Appleton, 1883)

Davis, W., *The Generals of the Civil War* (Mallard Press, 1992)

Dawes, R., *Service with the Sixth Wisconsin, Volunteers* (E.R. Alderman and Sons, 1890)

Donaldson, F. A., *Inside the Army of the Potomac: The Civil War Experience of Captain Francis Adams Donaldson* (Stackpole Books, 1998)

Doubleday, A., *Chancellorsville and Gettysburg, Vol. 6* (C. Scribner's Sons, 1882)

Duncan, R. R., *Beleaguered Winchester: A Virginia Community at War, 1861–1865* (LSU Press, 2007)

Early, J. A., *Lieutenant General Jubal Anderson Early, C.S.A* (J.B. Lippincott, 1912)

Eicher, D. J., *The Longest Night* (New York: Simon and Schuster, 2001)

Eicher, J. H., and David, J., *Civil War High Commands* (Stanford, C.A: Stanford University Press, 2001)

Fiebeger, G. J., *The Campaign and Battle of Gettysburg* (U.S. Military Academy Press, 1915)

Gilder, W., *The Century Illustrated Monthly Magazine, Vol. 86* (Scribner and Company, 1913)

Gleason, H. L., *A History of the First Regiment of Massachusetts Cavalry Volunteers* (Houghton: Mifflin and Company, 1891)

Gordon, J. B., *Reminiscences of the Civil War* (New York: Charles Scribner's Sons, The Martin and Hoyt Co., 1903)

Hard, A., *History of the Eighth Cavalry Regiment, Illinois Volunteers, During the Great Rebellion* (General Books LLC, 2010)

Hassler, W. W., *The First Day at Gettysburg: Crisis at the Crossroads* (University of Alabama Press, 2010); *One of Lee's Best Men: The Civil War Letters of General William Dorsey Pender* (UNC Press Books, 2012)

Hard, A., *The Road to Richmond: The Civil War Memoirs of Major Abner R. Small of the Sixteenth Maine Volunteers* (Fordham Unit Press, 1939)

Hefelbower, S. G., *The History of Gettysburg College* (Gettysburg College, 1932)

Hinkley, J., *Service with the Third Wisconsin Infantry* (Wisconsin History Commission, 1912)

Hoke, J., *Historical Reminiscences of the War* (M.A. Float, 1884); *The Great Invasion of 1863, or General Lee in Pennsylvania* (W.J. Shut, 1887)

Hotchkiss, J., *Make Me a Map of the Valley: The Civil War Journal of Stonewall Jackson's Topographer* (Southern Methodist University Press, 1973)

Howard, O. O., *Autobiography of Oliver Otis Howard, Major General, United States Army* (The Baker and Taylor Company, 1907)

Hunter, R., *Sketches of War History, 1861-1865: Papers Read Before the Ohio Commander of the Military Order of the Loyal Legion of the United States* (R. Clarke and Company, 1866)

Jones, J. W., *Personal Reminiscences, Anecdotes, and Letters of Gen. Robert E. Lee* (D. Appleton, 1875)

Martin, D. G., *Gettysburg, July 1* (Da Capo Press, 2003)

Jones, W., *Southern Historical Society Papers* (1877)

Kiefer, W., *History of the One Hundred and Fifty- Third Regiment Pennsylvania Volunteer Infantry* (Chemical Publishing Company, 1909)

McCellan, H. B., *The Life and Campaigns of Major General J. E. B. Stuart, Commander of the Cavalry of the Army of Northern Virginia* (Houghton: Mifflin Press, 1885)

McNeese, T., *Civil War Leaders* (Infobase Publishing, 2009)
Moore, F., *A Rebellion Record: A Diary of American Events with Documents, Narratives, Illustrative Incidents, Poetry, Etc, Vol. 7* (G.P. Putnam, 1864)
Mosby, J. S., *The Memoirs of Colonel John S. Mosby* (CreateSpace Independent Publishing Platform, 2015)
Mudge, A. *A History of the Class of 1854 in Dartmouth College Including Col. Haskell's Narrative of the Battle of Gettysburg* (Dartmouth College, 1898)
Myers, F. M., *The Commanches: A History of White's Battalion Virginia Cavalry* (Continental Book Company, 1871)
Nue, W., *Here Come the Rebels* (Morningside Bookshop, 1994)
O'Neill, R. F., *The Cavalry Battles of Allie, Middleburg, and Upperville: Small but Important Riots, June 10–27* (Lynchburg, Virginia: H.E. Howard, 1993)
Osborn, H., *Trials and Triumphs: The Record of the 55th Ohio Volunteer Infantry* (A.C. McClure and Company, 1904)
Pennypacker, S. W., *Historical and Biographical Sketches* (R.A. Tripple, 1883)
Petruzzi, D. J., *The Complete Gettysburg Guide* (Savas-Beatie LLC, 2009)
Pierce, J. V., *Final Report on the Battlefield of Gettysburg* (New York: J.B. Lyon Company Printers, 1902)
Pfanz, D. C., *The Letters of General Richard S. Ewell* (University of Tennessee Press, 2012)
Pfanz, H. W., *Gettysburg: The First Day* (UNC Press Books, 2011)
Salmon, J. S., *The Official Virginia Civil War Battlefield Guide* (Stackpole Books, 2001)
Sears, S. W., *Gettysburg* (Houghton: Mifflin Harcourt, 2004)
Smith, T., *Farms at Gettysburg: The Fields of Battle* (Thomas Publications, 2007)
Sorrel, G. M., *Recollections of a Confederate Staff Officer* (The Neale Publishing Company, 1905)
Stevenson, J. H., *Boots and Saddles: A History of the First Volunteer Cavalry of the War, Known as the First New York (Lincoln) Cavalry* (Patriot Publishing Company, 1879)
Thompson, J., *Reminiscences of Autauga Rifles* (J.M. Thompson, 1879)
Underwood, R., *Battles and Leaders of the Civil War: Being for the Most Part Contributions by Union and Confederate Officers, Vol. 3* (Century, 1888)
Wainwright, C. S., *A Diary of Battle: The Personal Journals of Colonel Charles S. Wainwright, 1861–1865* (Da Capo Press, 1998)
Walker, F., *History of the Second Army Corps in the Army of the Potomac, Vol. 2 Part 4* (C. Scribner's Sons, 1891)
Weld, S. M., *War Diary and Letters of Stephen Minot Weld, 1861–1865* (Cornell University Library)
Wert, J. D., *A Brotherhood of Valor: The Common Soldiers of the Stonewall Brigade C.S.A. and the "Iron Brigade" U.S.A* (Simon and Schuster, 2015)